the
LITTLE BOOK
of
AXOLOTL WISDOM

*live your life like the world's
weirdest, cutest salamander*

jessica allen

ULYSSES PRESS

Published by:
ULYSSES PRESS
PO Box 3440
Berkeley, CA 94703
www.ulyssespress.com

ISBN: 978-1-64604-417-7
Library of Congress Control Number: 2022936135

Printed in the United States by Versa Press
10 9 8 7 6 5 4 3 2 1

Acquisitions editor: Claire Sielaff
Managing editor: Claire Chun
Editor: Cathy Cambron
Proofreader: Barbara Schultz
Cover design and artwork: Kristine Byun
Layout: Winnie Liu and Yesenia Garcia-Lopez
Interior artwork: axolotls © Fandi Check/shutterstock.com

To Garrett, my mate for life

CONTENTS

INTRODUCTION

WHAT'S AN AXOLOTL?

In 1956, Julio Cortázar published a short story about a man who's so taken with axolotls that he transforms into one. If you've read the story, then there's a good chance that you, too, have fallen under the spell of the world's weirdest, cutest salamander. If not, you are about to be enchanted by these charming creatures, with their adorable baby faces and extraordinary ability to regenerate limbs and organs. While we can't promise that this book will turn you into an axolotl, we can promise that it will help you live a happier, healthier, saner life.

At first glance, we humans might not seem to have much in common with these large salamanders, native to a lake system near Mexico City. After all, we walk on two legs, have opposable thumbs, and can make multiple expressions using our mouths. We know how to whip up lattes and speak Mandarin. We invented corn dogs, computers, and cars.

An axolotl, on the other hand, has a big head, capped with a funky fringe that wouldn't be out of place at a Las Vegas revue. Its mouth cracks wide in a near-constant grin; its lidless eyes shine with iridescence. Attached to its long, squishy body are four limbs, with delicate fingers and toes, and an extensive, flexible tail. The overall effect is a bit bonkers, like a cartoon come to life.

But, as you'll soon discover, what axolotls lack in physical sophistication they more than make up for in attitude. They are masters of resilience, models of cheerful stoicism. We have a lot to learn from these amphibians.

The Aztec were so taken with these animals that they incorporated axolotls into their mythology, nicknaming them "water dogs" and extolling their impish spirit. They remain an important part of Mexico's identity, even appearing on the back of the 50-peso bill (part of the reason this currency was named 2021 Banknote of the Year by the International Bank Note Society).

Much of what we know about axolotls comes from more than 200 years of scientific research. This research has required some nasty business, such as repeatedly removing a specimen's leg just to watch it grow back again and again and again and again (for more on that amazing power, see axiom 12 on page 47). Axolotls are among the most successful animals used in laboratory settings, and their genome might hold the key to curing cancer and other diseases.

Successful as axolotls have been in labs, they're critically endangered in the wild. The last count, in 2019, found fewer than 1,000 in their native habitat. Even as we admire the axolotl's spirit and learn more about its babyishness (known as neoteny), we have a responsibility to help preserve these amphibians' environment so that they can be enjoyed for generations to come. Thankfully, plenty of folks agree, including the developers of Minecraft, who introduced an axolotl mob to the game in 2021 to bring attention to this salamander's current path to extinction and encourage conservation efforts.

FAST FACTS

- ♡ **Pronunciation:** ACKS-oh-lot-ul (rhymes with "packs-a-bottle")
- ♡ **Scientific name:** *Ambystoma mexicanum*
- ♡ **Class:** Amphibia
- ♡ **Life span (in the wild):** 10–15 years
- ♡ **Habitat:** Lake Xochimilco (near Mexico City)
- ♡ **Size:** up to 12 inches
- ♡ **Weight:** 2–8 ounces
- ♡ **Diet:** carnivorous
- ♡ **Nickname:** Mexican walking fish*

Kind of a weird nickname, to be honest, since axolotls aren't fish and don't walk on land. But giving yourself a fierce or beautiful nickname isn't a bad idea. See axiom 2 on page 17 for the reason.

WHAT'S AN "AXOLOTL AXIOM"?

At the heart of this book are 31 *axolotl axioms*. An axolotl axiom is a guiding principle, designed to help you live a smarter, sweeter, more fun-filled existence. We rely on facts, from biology to psychology to sociology to zoology, and we offer practical, actionable tips to help you discover and live your best life. Take what speaks to you, and leave the rest behind—after all, that's totally what an axolotl would do. Each axiom is marked by an icon:

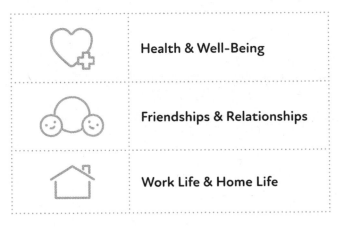

	Health & Well-Being
	Friendships & Relationships
	Work Life & Home Life

In the Health & Well-Being section, you'll find advice and axolotl facts related to taking care of yourself (physically and mentally), dealing with stress, breathing better, and making good choices. This is the largest section because our health and well-being have such an impact on every other aspect of our lives.

The Friendships & Relationships section deals with family, friends, and romantic partners. Here, we'll talk about being a good listener and a good conversationalist, broadening your mind, setting boundaries, and showing affection the axolotl way. Axolotls need people to help preserve their habitat. Same goes for humans—we need one another to give our lives richness and emotional depth.

Not surprisingly, Work Life & Home Life axioms offer advice about dealing with careers, school, hobbies, and your environment. From tips on organizing your life, to having a cause you care about, to using rituals to beat back procrastination, these axioms are designed to help you create a cozy, solid base from which to navigate the wider world.

We are connected to the world around us in a variety of ways. Or, as Roman emperor Marcus Aurelius wrote in the second century: "As Marcus, I have Rome, and as a human being I have the universe." Feeling good about yourself puts good into the world. And our world could always use more good.

Of course, axolotls are nothing if not joyful and beguiling. They just might be the ideal remedy for our wrung-out, worn-out collective soul. If they can survive and often thrive in new circumstances, then so can we. We hope you find axolotls as inspiring as we do.

Following the advice in this book will make you approximately 600 times cuter. However, this book is not meant to treat, prevent, or diagnose any disease or condition, nor is it meant as a substitute for medical advice. Some issues require professional help. Please make an appointment to speak with your doctor if you're at all concerned. It's what an axolotl would do!

AXOLOTL
AXIOMS

REMEMBER THAT YOU ARE A MIRACLE

Being a paleontologist is harder than Ross makes it look on *Friends*. You have to know where to dig, then do the actual digging. And you have to be able to tell the difference between regular rocks and valuable ones that might hold the secret of life within their layers. Challenging work coupled with luck—it's incredible that anything ever gets found.

A paleontologist's work is even harder when it comes to ancient salamanders. With their delicate little bones, salamanders haven't contributed much to the fossil record. So it was a big deal when scientists in 2020 reported the discovery of a 230-million-year-old fossil, the earliest known salamander, in Kyrgyzstan. This specimen of *Triassurus sixtelae* will help scientists more fully understand how amphibians evolved.

Fast-forward from this ancestor several millennia and head about 8,200 miles west. Approximately 10,000 years ago, in the spring-fed waters of central Mexico, a creature with a cute face, a ginormous grin, and the power to repeatedly regrow its limbs, brain, and organs split from another species called the tiger salamander. Said creature has since endured habitat degradation and scientific experimentation. It's been declared extinct, only to continue to survive in the wild and to positively flourish in laboratories. Miraculous, right?

Yes! The axolotl is a miracle, and so are you. Somehow you arrived on this planet at this particular time. Cells clung together to form organisms that crawled out of the ooze, avoided being eaten, reproduced, and evolved, in due time, into humans. Those humans had humans who had humans who had humans who moved to Minneapolis or Montreal or Mogadishu and made you. Whoever you are, wherever you're from, wherever you're headed, you're the only you who has ever existed. Isn't that amazing?

We live in remarkable times; wonders are invented and discovered every day. With their big embryos, long genomes, and powers of regeneration, axolotls have enormous potential to help scientists make major advances in medicine, including finding a cure for cancer (see axiom 4 on page 23 for more information about axolotls' contributions to scientific study). We have much to celebrate—and anticipate.

Of course, the world isn't all bingeworthy TV, no-cal cheesecakes, and full-body virtual reality suits. Although human history is full of horrors, our era seems worse—perhaps because it's ours. None of us asked to be born; none of us chose the situation we were born into. Yet, here we are. It's up to us to leave the world better than we found it (see axiom 25 on page 86 for reasons you should pick a cause). Goodness knows, we have plenty of role models. We're looking at you, Greta Thunberg, Dolores Huerta, and Malala Yousafzai—among many others.

Treat yourself like the miracle you are. Take care of yourself by exercising, eating right, and getting regular checkups. Wear a seatbelt, wear a helmet, look both ways, practice safer sex, and always read the fine print. Develop healthy habits. Be kind, not critical. Miracles are precious, and so are you. Guard your time; guard your joy. Know your worth. Expect to be treated like the miracle you are. And be sure to treat other people—and our astonishing planet—like the miracles they are.

BE A WOOPER LOOPER

In the 13th century, the people we know as the Aztec began moving into what is now central Mexico. They called themselves the Mexica, and they called the salamanders they discovered axolotls. In the original Nahuatl, an Aztec language, *axolotl* means "water sprite," "water monster," "water doll," or "water dog" (translations differ). Not coincidentally, Xolotl, the Aztec god associated with axolotls (see axiom 3 on page 20), was often portrayed as having a dog head.

A 16th-century naturalist took one look at axolotls and termed them *piscis ludicrous*, or "ludicrous fish." He was half-right—axolotls are nothing if not absurd-looking. These days, axolotls are sometimes known as "Mexican walking fish," although they don't walk on land and aren't fish. But the best name for axolotls is from

Japan, where they're called "wooper loopers"—a *kawaii* name for a *kawaii* critter.

While names can be hurtful, they can also be inspiring and empowering. In her prose poem "Difficult Names," Warsan Shire writes, "Give your daughters difficult names. Give your daughters names that command the full use of tongue." Names can confer authority and demand respect. The poem continues: "My name makes you want to tell me the truth. My name doesn't allow me to trust anyone that cannot pronounce it right." Names are inextricably linked to identity. Think about the names you use for yourself. Be honest. Names are potent, as Shire describes. Call yourself a name that truly reflects who you are and what you want. Tell everyone, or tell no one.

Once you've given yourself a name, think about the names other people call you or the names you wish they'd call you. Correct people who mispronounce your name. If a childhood nickname no longer reflects you, politely request that it be retired. What's cute at 4 could be demeaning at 14 or 40.

In recent years, our culture has witnessed a sea change in the use of names. People proudly bear labels related to their ethnicity, religion, or heritage that they might once have rejected. New terms have been invented, and new names adopted, to better portray a range of gender identities and expressions. We have more power to define ourselves than ever before—let's use it. There's no need to default.

Selecting labels works in other realms as well, particularly with regard to Future You and Career You. Assuming you're putting in the work, go ahead and call yourself whatever it is you wish to be. You don't have to be a best-selling author to call yourself a writer, clock a four-minute mile to call yourself a runner, or discover a galaxy to call yourself an astronomer.

The key is putting in the work. If your sneakers are gathering dust in the back of your closet, then you can't refer to yourself as a runner, no matter how much you wish you were. Some labels require professional certification, and misrepresenting yourself can be unethical or illegal. But no committee decides when someone gets to be a baker, gamer, golfer, artist, singer, stylist, content creator, backpacker, or a million other things. Add such labels, as well as your nickname and pronouns, to your social handles. If it feels more authentic, add "future": *future doctor, future entrepreneur, future real estate mogul.* Share your selves with the world. Be a wooper looper.

KNOW YOUR ROOTS

While building their great capital city of Tenochtitlan, the Aztec became quite taken with the axolotl. These salamanders made their way into Aztec art and mythology, notably through an association with Xolotl, god of fire and lightning, guide to the underworld, and twin of Quetzalcoatl, among the most revered beings in the Mesoamerican pantheon.

According to the Aztec creation myth known as "The Raising of the Fifth Sun," Xolotl needed to die so that the moon and the sun could travel across the sky. Understandably not keen on being sacrificed, he cried so much that his eyes fell out of their sockets. Xolotl attempted to avoid capture by turning himself into different plants and animals. The axolotl was Xolotl's final disguise before he was discovered and slain.

In stories, both axolotls and Xolotl were considered rebellious, impish, and mischievous. While Xolotl did his duty as deity, axolotl tamales became a staple of the Aztec diet. Despite his ultimate end, the Aztec associated Xolotl with transformation.

Every one of us has an origin story, and it begins at the cellular level. Our genes determine such physical characteristics as eye color, blood type, nose size, hair color, and freckles. Genes regulate whether we can roll our tongue and which thumb naturally goes on top when we clasp our hands together. They predispose us to a host of health conditions, including high cholesterol, alcoholism, dementia, asthma, heart disease, and diabetes. We say that things "run in the family," because lots of things do. The apple doesn't fall all that far from the tree.

Genetics aren't the only powerful forces helping shape who we are. Our origin story also encompasses our childhood, from experiences to memories to various figures whom we revered or reviled. If your big brother was a huge Eagles fan, then perhaps you are as well. Or you may trace your green thumb to a day care teacher who taught you to grow an avocado plant from a pit. And if your parents struggled with addiction, you might want to exercise caution.

On the flip side, you might want to call your family and thank them for giving you a love of woodworking, teaching you how to use a sprocket wrench, taking you on international trips, paying for college, or encouraging your athletic ability. Knowing your roots—good and not-so-good—brings insight.

This insight is incredibly useful. We can mitigate genetic tendencies through exercise and regular health screens. We can fill out those lengthy forms about family history at our doctor's office honestly and without complaining. Similarly, we can recognize psychological proclivities or address deep-seated feelings through therapy, journaling, and good old-fashioned talking to friends. We can acknowledge our privilege. Without knowledge, there can be no transformation.

Biology doesn't have to be destiny, and our fates aren't fixed. It takes effort and energy to dig around in the past, most definitely, but also to avoid getting stuck repeatedly reliving messy moments. Understanding is effective; wallowing is not. When done with an open heart and clear eyes, reflecting on where we come from helps us figure out where we're headed—and whether it's advisable to consider a detour.

BELIEVE SCIENCE

In 1925, surrealists in Paris developed a collaborative game they called *cadavre exquis* ("exquisite corpse"). As André Breton, Marcel Duchamp, and their pals conceived of it, participants would contribute drawings to a piece of paper without being able to see what else was on it. The result, as you might imagine, was often jumbled and disconnected, particularly as *le vin* started to flow.

Axolotls look like the kind of animal drunk poets and artists would invent at a party: piebald or pink, with an uber-bendable body, frilly mane, and easygoing smile. But that friendly, far-out appearance belongs to one of the world's most seriously studied creatures.

Enumerating the axolotl's contributions to science over the past 200+ years would take volumes. Well-known and often used in laboratories, axolotls have helped scientists to do all these things and more:

- ♡ Understand how organs grow and behave in vertebrates
- ♡ Figure out what causes spina bifida (a birth defect that leads to spinal malformation in humans)
- ♡ Discover thyroid hormones and advance endocrinology
- ♡ Explore evolutionary history
- ♡ Analyze environmental adaptations (especially in relation to the retention of juvenile characteristics into adulthood, a phenomenon we discuss in axiom 30 on page 101)
- ♡ Investigate neurodegenerative diseases (such as Alzheimer's)
- ♡ Make inroads into regenerative medicine and gene therapy

Axolotls have one of the largest embryos of any amphibian, and those embryos are themselves filled with large cells. Their size and varied pigmentation have enabled scientists to better understand stem cells, including the development of embryonic tissues and organs.

While investigating axolotl embryos, Dr. Crystal Rogers has made the animals at her UC Davis School of Veterinary Medicine lab internet-famous. The Rogers Lab relies on #ChonkTheAxolotl and siblings to learn more about the molecular mechanisms and environmental factors that influence vertebrate development. "Come for Chonk, stay for the science," her website says.

Although an axolotl might resemble an uncooked chicken breast, it has one of the world's biggest genomes—some 10 times larger than ours. Thanks to the axolotl, scientists have developed advanced techniques for gene assembly. Nestled within an axolotl's 32 billion base pairs of DNA are more than 90 gene sequences that aren't found in birds, reptiles, or mammals.

Genome sequence in hand, scientists have begun searching for the molecular key to the axolotl's powers of regeneration (see axiom 12 on page 47). Being able to regrow damaged organs and limbs is of immense interest to scientists—limb difference and limb loss, particularly from accidents and diabetes, affects more than 2 million Americans a year. The US Department of Defense is also eager to understand the process, and has invested millions to do so.

In addition, axolotls are thought to be 1,000 times more resistant to cancer than humans. Somewhere inside these smiley salamanders might be tools to fight or cure this devastating disease. One thing seems certain: axolotls will continue to contribute to scientific breakthroughs.

Over the past few years, anti-science aggression—consisting of deliberate attempts to discredit scientifically validated research and verifiable facts—has been mounting in the United States. This dangerous trend has popped up in places from social media to the dinner table to debates over federal laws and funding. When confronted with fallacious reasoning or outright falsehoods, remember the humble axolotl and all it has done, and continues to do, to further scientific knowledge.

BREATHE BETTER

One of the axolotl's most noticeable characteristics is the freaky fringe framing its face. This fringe lends the axolotl a distinctive cartoonishness. It's also relaxing to watch the feathery fronds sway almost tenderly in the water. But beneath the cuteness is a serious purpose: this distinctive headgear is actually a series of external gill stalks (three on each side), known as *rami*. Oxygen in the water passes through the gills' thin skin and goes straight to the axolotl's bloodstream.

Salamanders start out in the water, emerging from eggs and using gills to breathe. As their lungs start to develop, salamanders gradually transition from an aquatic youth to an adulthood on land, much as young adult humans leave their childhood homes to establish their own abodes. Axolotls, however, are a little different. Although they grow functional lungs, axolotls spend their entire lives in water, never maturing to a terrestrial existence (see axiom 30 on page 101 to learn more about neoteny).

Because axolotls have functional, albeit primitive lungs, they sometimes head to the surface and breathe in air. In other words, they have different ways of breathing, even if they rely on one mechanism more than the other. Unlike axolotls, humans have only lungs. Nevertheless, we can use the axolotl breathing switch-eroo as a reminder to focus on our own breath.

Have you ever been so stressed you could barely breathe? Short, spiky breaths give us an advantage in times of danger. The trouble is that many of us live on short, spiky breaths. We tend to take rather shallow breaths most of the time, which keeps our sympathetic nervous system on high alert.

Diaphragmatic breathing—in which you draw breath from the nose down into the belly—is better. Go ahead and take a full, big breath now. I'll wait.

Breathing is as unconscious a process for us as it is for axolotls. Yet, by deliberately slowing down our breath and moving it deeper into our bodies, we can give ourselves tremendous benefits. We can activate the parasympathetic nervous system, explains James Nestor in his best-selling book *Breath: The New Science of a Lost Art*. We can chill ourselves out.

There are many different methods for initiating diaphragmatic breathing. One of the most common, known as box breath, works like this: inhale for four counts, hold on full for four counts, exhale for four counts, hold on empty for four counts. If that feels like too much, take it to two counts. Aim for four to six rounds.

Another technique is called five-finger, or hand, breathing: spread one hand in front of you, then use the index finger of your other hand to trace each finger of the outstretched hand, inhaling as you go up and exhaling as you go down.

To get your body more involved, try elevator breath: start standing, bent at the waist, with your hands and head pointed toward the floor (like forward fold in yoga). As you rise up, slowly breathe in until you're standing straight and tall with full lungs (like mountain pose in yoga). Then gradually fold back down, exhaling as you go.

What's great about breathing is that it's always available to you. Taking a few seconds to focus on your breath slows everything down, allowing you to transition from an attitude of "oh my gosh, everything's on FIRE!!!!!!!!!!!!!!!!" to a calm place. Staying even-keeled is much easier when you're breathing deeply.

6

KNOW YOUR NEEDS

In 1943, psychologist Abraham Maslow published a "hierarchy of needs" to explain what people require to thrive and be their best selves. This hierarchy is often represented as a five-level pyramid—although, interestingly, Maslow didn't conceive of it as such. The most essential needs (food, water, shelter) are at the bottom; then come safety needs, social needs, esteem needs; and, at the very top, self-actualization.

Axolotl needs are fairly basic: calm, clean water, and a good supply of their favorite foods, such as insects. As ectothermic (cold-blooded) animals, their internal body temperature is regulated by their environment. If an axolotl needs to feel less cold when the temperature drops, it might swim or walk along the lake bottom to get to a warmer spot, where it will hang out and hunt.

Maslow's work offers a useful paradigm for our lives. Once your primary needs for things like safety and shelter are met, what do you need for optimal function? Is it nine hours of sleep every night (learn more about sleep in axiom 11 on page 44), a regular phone call with your mom, an evening walk?

To understand your needs, begin by filling in the blanks:

♡ I'm the type of person who _____

♡ I'm happiest when I _____

♡ I'm calmest when I _____

♡ I feel strong when I _____

This activity isn't about being critical or aspirational. Rather, it's about accepting and understanding yourself. Being honest about your needs isn't always easy, but it's worth the effort. Self-knowledge can help you be a better friend, sibling, child, partner, citizen, and person. Only you can answer those questions, and only you can figure out how to be the best you.

I am a fully functioning adult by anyone's measure. To wit: I have feelings about the right stock/bond split for retirement. I'm a card-carrying member of the Parent Teacher Association. I have legit thrown out my back multiple times. And, yet, I eat a lot of candy—as in every single day.

Sure, candy isn't the same as oxygen or a place to live, but it's a need that pops up for me after the essentials have been covered.

Maslow stressed *self*-actualization (emphasis mine), because what populates the top of anyone's pyramid is unique to that person. In my world, everything's better on days with candy.

Part of being a grown-up is letting go of other people's expectations. We're bombarded with "shoulds," "oughts," and "musts" from a variety of social, cultural, and familial sources. Understanding yourself enables you to tune out the noise about what you should do, how you should dress, where you should live, and who you really are. Trust yourself to know yourself.

Of course, another big part of being an adult is doing stuff you don't feel like doing. Them's the breaks, as they say. I *want* to spend all my money on candy, but I *need* to save some money for candy in retirement. I can't wait to sample future candy—will it be made on the moon and come with tiny jet packs?

Knowing your needs also necessitates that you acknowledge that other people might have different needs (discover more about broadening your mind in axiom 19 on page 68). In keeping with my food metaphor, you don't want to yuck someone else's yum. My candy obsession is your love of kale. In the grocery store of life, there's room for us all.

7

UNDERREACT

Looking at an axolotl, with its goofy smile and funky headgear, it's hard to imagine how aggressive these creatures can be. And, yet, they have been known to eat one another in the wild and in laboratories. Their limbs end in surprisingly human-like digits capped with tiny claws, which they don't hesitate to use. They might appear affable, and most of the time they are, but they can turn nasty.

Aggressively as axolotls sometimes behave, they've got nothing on us. Over the course of human history, it's estimated that between 150 million and 1 billion people have been killed in wars. That's to say nothing of other types of violence, trauma, and inhumanity. We are, by far, the most dangerous animals on the planet.

Scientists manage axolotl tendencies by keeping different sized animals in separate cages. In the wild, unless they've just been born or are mating, axolotls tend to avoid one another, limiting potentially explosive situations. We can lessen our own bellicose tendencies by underreacting.

Anger begets anger; aggression begets aggression. This escalating effect is one reason screaming into a pillow might make you feel worse, not better. It's why the irritation of stubbing your toe in the morning can lead you to flip someone off on your commute, and from there snowball into an argument with a coworker or a fight with your partner later that day.

When it comes to controlling our reactions and dealing with stress, therapists talk about the 5x5 Rule: if something won't matter in five years, don't spend more than five minutes thinking about it. Speaking of fives, here's another adage to keep in mind: don't have a five-dollar reaction to a five-cent problem.

Life offers us seemingly no end of five-cent problems (a.k.a. irritating situations). In his second-century *Meditations*, a Stoic self-help and advice book, Roman emperor Marcus Aurelius put it this way: "Do unsavory armpits and bad breath make you angry? What good will it do you?"

You can absolutely get angry about stinky armpits, traffic, your friend's habit of clearing her throat before stating an opinion, the way the coffee shop that's closest to work forgets to restock the oat milk, and on and on. You can put out your claws and react with hostility. Overreaction is an available option, sure. Just be prepared for the aforementioned snowball effect: the more irritated we get, the less patience we have, and the harder it is to modulate our reaction when the next thing goes wrong. Being reactive impedes our power to pay attention and respond appropriately.

Alternatively, you can channel Marcus Aurelius and think about what purpose your anger serves in that moment. You might conjure Elsa in *Frozen*, fling out your arms, and "let it goooooooooooo." Multiple octaves aside, that's underreacting in action. No oat milk? Okay. At least you have money to spend on coffee and a job to go to. And your throat-clearing friend? At least you have a buddy with interesting opinions to share. Things could certainly be worse.

Along with a plethora of five-cent problems, life offers plenty of five-dollar problems. Learning to recognize the difference can be a challenge (see axiom 14 on page 53 for info about fact-checking your feelings). We can't control what comes into our lives, but we can control ourselves, including our reactions. By ignoring the irritants, we store up our emotional energy for true emergencies.

KILL YOUR INNER CRITIC

Picture this: you're at a party when the host introduces you to C. Immediately, C begins complaining about the wait for drinks (too long), the living room furniture (too beige), the music (too loud). C turns to you. Starting with your face, body, hair, and outfit, then moving on to your personality, C catalogs your flaws, maybe throwing in a few memories of past mistakes for good measure.

Desperate to escape, you scan the room and see an axolotl. The party instantly becomes 10 times better! In the wild, this axolotl would probably be brown, black, or olive, all the better to camouflage itself; if bred in captivity, its color might be creamy white with saffron-colored spots or a pale millennial pink. Regardless, the axolotl blissfully sways its tail to the beat.

At an actual party, you'd likely do whatever you could to get away from the soul-sucking C and head over to the axolotl section. However, all too often, we welcome C—short for Critical Critic—into our minds. We let this inner critic steal our attention and our joy, giving C a spotlight and a microphone, instead of the heave-ho.

One way to slay your inner critic is to offer yourself an infusion of confidence. Recall a time when you achieved a goal or met with success. Make a list of your special strengths. If you're having trouble coming up with a list, think about what a friend or parent would say. Clinical social worker Leslie Herhold recommends pairing each strength with the phrase "I am": *I am enthusiastic, I am imaginative, I am determined.*

The inner critic loves the past. Ruminating on poor choices or errors in judgment gets C's engine going. The fact is, we are not who we once were. We're constantly changing, no matter how old we are. Life offers zillions of occasions for trying harder and doing better—the growth mindset applies to adults as well as kids.

Your inner critic differs from my inner critic, but both likely spend a fair amount of time opining on our shape and size. Body positivity—the belief that all bodies are beautiful and worthy of celebration—can help counter harmful messages from the media and foster a sense of acceptance. According to body neutrality, bodies aren't bad or good; they merely are. This belief shifts the conversation from what a body looks like to what it can do, like hugging a loved one or hiking a mountain. If your body were a car, then you might take pride in its curves and sleek hood, or you might see it as a way to get wherever you want to go. Either philosophy does a great job of combating the inner critic.

Muzzling the critical monologue requires radical self-compassion and self-love. You have to be your own best friend. Sometimes you, or your real-life bestie, has to give you a stern talk. Just remember that your inner critic isn't the same thing as your conscience. When your conscience comes knocking, open the door and listen. If the inner critic gets loud, you need to turn up some other tune, such as a mantra. Your mantra doesn't need to be fancy. It can be as simple as the one Michelle Obama discusses in her memoir *Becoming*: "Am I good enough? Yes, I am."

STAY HYDRATED

Amphibious axolotls spend their lives in water (we talk more about this evolutionary adaptation in axiom 30 page 101). But do aquatic creatures such as axolotls drink the water they live in?

The answer is "it depends." Dolphins and other marine mammals, for instance, usually get water from their food and by internal metabolic processes, not by drinking seawater. Sharks, in contrast, take in seawater through their gills. Alligators swim to the surface and drink rainwater. Many species of fish drink a lot of water and, as a result, pee a lot. Fish—they're just like us!

Amphibians, including axolotls, need a wet environment to survive, yet they don't usually drink water. Instead, they absorb water through their skin. They may ingest some water while eating, too.

Human bodies contain a fair amount of water: our brain is approximately 73 percent water, our lungs closer to 83 percent. We lose water as we age—a human baby is almost 80 percent water, an adult woman about 55 percent.

Water helps us digest food, brings oxygen and nutrients to our cells, regulates our body temperature, lubricates our joints, and cushions our spinal cord. We lose water through sweat, urine, bowel movements, and breath. Every exhalation contains a small amount of water vapor (water in gas form), along with carbon dioxide, which is why we can see our breath when it's cold. The interaction between the cold air and warm water vapor transforms the latter into a liquid or even a solid.

Cool, cool, cool, you say. But how much water do we need to drink? Does the old adage about eight glasses a day hold? Again, the answer is "it depends."

People who are pregnant or breastfeeding need more water, as do people who've been exercising. Kids need more water than grown-ups. You tend to need more water in the summer or in hotter climates.

On average, we should be drinking four to six eight-ounce cups of water per day. If you often feel thirsty, or your urine is very dark or has a strong smell, you might not be getting enough water. Up your intake of fluids; eat some juicy, water-filled fruits and veggies, such as watermelon and cucumber; and make an appointment with your doctor to rule out other causes.

A glass of water is a miracle cure. So often, what we attribute to other things—stress, tiredness, lack of caffeine, the Sunday scaries—can be alleviated with a glass of water. The act of drinking water serves another purpose, in addition to keeping you hydrated: it gives you time to think. This pause is especially important when you're frantic, enabling you to modulate your reactions (as we discuss in axiom 7 on "Underreact" on page 32), and fact-check your feelings (see axiom 14 on page 53). A few sips help you reset.

The next time you take a drink of water, contemplate this: the planet's water cycle has existed for 3.8 billion years. The same water is (re)cycled, from clouds to rain to rivers and reservoirs, over and over. Very little has evaporated into space during all that time. In other words, the water you're drinking could have been splashed in by a T. rex. Water's not just hydrating—it's mind-blowing!

NURTURE AWE

Science journalist Feini Yin once described the axolotl as a "cheerful tube sock." That's among the cutest—and most accurate—descriptions I've ever read of this silly-looking salamander. It's no wonder that the Pokémon Axolil is based on the axolotl (see Famous Axolotls on page 109).

If you're anything like me, an axolotl's mien probably makes you go "awwwwwww." And once you've read about its humongous genome, its ability to regenerate, and its survival despite challenging circumstances, you can't help but be awed.

Awe is an often-misunderstood emotion. On the one hand, it's frequently associated with unbridled enthusiasm and naivete about the world. To be awed is to be easily impressed and goofily slack-jawed. Not only is awe uncool, it can come off as tone-deaf. It's hard, and maybe borderline inappropriate, to feel awe on days when the world seems headed for the toilet.

On the other hand, being awed can be awesome. The title of a 2012 research study led by marketing professor Melanie Rudd says it all: "Awe Expands People's Perception of Time, Alters Decision Making, and Enhances Well-Being." Awe has been found to combat depression and reduce anxiety. Another study found a connection between positive emotions and better health.

Along with eating right, exercising, and getting enough sleep, experiencing awe can help you live longer. Suddenly, standing slack-jawed seems kind of rad. Awe is an antidote to negativity, fretfulness, and anger. It invigorates you to solve problems and tackle crises.

Nevertheless, getting to a state of awe isn't always easy. The phrase "there is nothing new under the sun" comes from the Bible, specifically Ecclesiastes 1:9. So, basically, the "been there, done that" attitude is older than Christianity.

For an axolotl, awe is a piece of cake. An axolotl's face has a permanent expression of awe, since axolotls don't blink and mostly swim around with their mouths hanging open, hoping some food will float in. They appear to exist in a perpetual state of wide-eyed amazement.

Daily drudgery can seriously impede our access to awe. Here are some shortcuts:

- ♡ Go outside. Wherever you live, nature offers pure awesomeness. I once watched a raptor dive-bomb a pigeon in the middle of Manhattan.

- ♡ Rethink technology. Imagine your great-grandmother's reaction to your smartphone or your washer-dryer combo. Much of the tech we take for granted in our lives is absolutely incredible.

- ♡ Break an experience into little parts. Listen carefully to a Lizzo song, and separate the vocals from the instrumentals. Note every beat, every pause. Admire how she plays the flute (she's named her favorites Sasha, after Beyoncé's alter ego, Sasha Fierce, and Blue, after Beyoncé's daughter Blue Ivy).

- ♡ Write it down. The Greater Good Science Center at the University of California, Berkeley, recommends an "awe narrative," in which you describe a time when you felt profound wonder, reverence, or astonishment.

We associate awe with nature, art, and spirituality, and rightly so. From the star-filled sky of the countryside to a sweeping orchestral arrangement by Beethoven to the golden gorgeousness of Kinkaku-ji (a Zen Buddhist temple in Kyoto), awe surrounds us. If all else fails, access awe by contemplating your own miraculous self (see axiom 1 on page 14).

GET GOOD SLEEP

During the day, axolotls typically snuggle into mud, camouflage themselves in vegetation, or otherwise do what they can to avoid predators. As with humans, the level of activity among axolotls varies. In fact, some axolotls have been described as lazy, inactive, and even dormant.

Scientists have yet to find an animal who doesn't sleep. Creatures from fruit flies to falcons to the Florida panther engage in a period of stillness and quietness (that is, sleep). Sleeping is thought to help conserve energy, activate rejuvenation and necessary growth processes, and increase brain plasticity. For humans, anyway, it's also a fun way to see what's happening in your subconscious via your dreams. Have you had the one with Jason Momoa eating a hot fudge sundae while riding a unicorn? No? Maybe that's just me.

You can be sure that axolotls are getting their necessary hours of shut-eye. As for humans? Eh, not so much. For many of us, getting by on the minimum number of hours of sleep has become a badge of honor. We brag about how little sleep we need in the same breath as we extol our multiple side hustles. Rather than resist the productivity trap (see axiom 31 on page 104), we fall into it, stretch out, and make our bed there. Then we suffer major consequences.

Everyone knows what it's like to get a poor night's sleep. You feel sluggish and tired. Every molehill looms like a mountain. Your brain seems foggy and addled. Perhaps you power through with a coffee, and perhaps you do it again the next day and the day after that. Some of us sleepwalk through the work week, only to try to "catch up" on the weekends.

The problem is that we can never really catch up. Sleep deprivation is both real and cumulative. Not getting enough sleep leads to cognitive impairment and memory loss.

And it gets worse. Recent studies have shown that consistently getting fewer than six hours per night in your 50s and 60s can lead to dementia. Adults of all ages who don't get enough sleep tend to be obese and can develop diabetes or have problems with alcohol, possibly as a result of being literally too tired to make good choices.

In short, sleep and sleep hygiene matter. How much sleep you need depends on your age. Preschoolers need more than teenagers, who need more than adults. The American Academy of Sleep Medicine offers a Bedtime Calculator that tells you the optimal time to go to sleep based on your age and typical wake-up time. Generally, though, teens need eight to ten hours and adults need at least seven hours.

A caveat: As with everything, there are some sleep outliers. Not everyone needs a lot of sleep. Since 2009, scientists have identified at least three "short sleep" genes. People with these genes appear to be able to function on fewer than six hours, with no ill effects. For every Gwyneth Paltrow, who aims for 10 hours of shut-eye, there's a Tom Ford, who gets by on around four hours a night.

To capture the big benefits of beauty rest, put your phone in another room (no more sleeping with it under your pillow!). Avoid big meals and caffeine before bedtime. Try to go to bed and wake up at the same time every day. Close your eyes. Instead of sheep, count axolotls, gently gliding, fringe softly undulating.

HARNESS YOUR GROWTH FACTOR

Cut off an axolotl's leg, and it regrows. Chop off a toe, and the toe returns. Do it again and again and again—and the missing part will come back, same as before, as if the injury never happened. Although this regenerative ability sounds like something out of the Marvel Universe, it's totally real.

When it comes to axolotls, nothing is more astonishing than this power of regeneration. An axolotl can regrow its limbs, muscles, eyes, tail, jaw—even a crushed spinal cord and parts of its brain, lungs, and heart. Axolotls can do this at any age and can repeat the wound-regrowth cycle at least five times.

After a wound, a group of cells known as a *blastema* gathers at the injury site. In humans, the blastema forms scar tissue. In axolotls, though, the blastema mimics cells in an embryo. Some cells turn off their old instructions and begin forming new muscle, bone, and tissue. Others keep their identity but begin multiplying. Working together, the cells replace precisely what's been lost or damaged, which is the reason an axolotl who's missing a right foreleg will regrow a right foreleg, not a left foreleg or 14 more legs. This new leg will be the correct structure, size, and shape.

Scientists are studying the axolotl genome to learn more about how regeneration occurs. They know that it relies, in part, on "growth factors," or proteins that foster tissue development. We have growth factors, too. If you've ever cut yourself or gotten sunburned, then you've regrown skin. Until scientists figure out exactly how axolotls regenerate, we humans remain limited in our ability to physically repair ourselves. However, we have an enormous internal capacity for resilience.

Grit and resilience go hand in hand, yet they are technically separate concepts. As researchers have defined these terms, grit has to do with persisting, persevering, and striving for a goal. Regardless of failure or hardship, your dedication to achieving the goal doesn't waiver. You own your hard (see axiom 13 on page 50). Grit is Albert Einstein saying, "It's not that I'm so smart, it's just that I stay with problems longer." While grit is about the doing, resilience is about the thinking. Resilience has to do with attitude and mental health. When you're resilient, you believe in yourself. You know you can do hard things. Being resilient doesn't mean being tough; it means being able to bounce back after challenges.

It doesn't mean never falling down (because everybody falls down occasionally); it means having enough energy and mental fortitude to get back up.

Sometimes knowing someone else believes in you is enough to help you harness your growth factor. For example, Stephen King attributes much of his success to his wife's unwavering support. After King gave up on the first draft of *Carrie*, she took the pages out of the trash and urged him to continue. The result went on to sell millions of copies and launched his career as one of the world's most popular writers.

If we're lucky enough to have a Tabitha King in our lives, we owe that person thanks, as King well knows: *Carrie* is dedicated to his wife. (See axiom 21 on page 74 for more about choosing a partner.) But, even if we don't, we can be our own Tabithas. We can channel this kind of support and cultivate resilience. We can love ourselves. Maybe we can adopt a mantra to recite whenever we need a boost: *I am fierce and fabulous*, *I am a miracle*, or *I got this*. I offer you the words of my favorite yoga teacher, who often ends class by saying, "I love you. Keep going."

OWN YOUR HARD

The destruction of the axolotl habitat began with the arrival of Hernán Cortés to Mexico in 1519. As part of their conquest of the Aztec, the Spanish drained many of the lakes around Tenochtitlan. Draining continued until the mid-20th century, when Mexico City's rapid urbanization began putting pressure on Xochimilco and its eponymous lake, the last remaining habitat of wild axolotls.

A 1998 survey by Academia Mexicana de Ciencias (Mexican Academy of Sciences) found 6,000 axolotls, on average, for each square kilometer. By 2003, that figure had decreased to 1,000; by 2008, the average number of axolotls in that range had fallen to 100. According to data collected in 2019 by the International Union for Conservation of Nature, the world's leading conservationist

THE LITTLE BOOK OF AXOLOTL WISDOM

body, fewer than 1,000 axolotls are left in the wild, making these amphibians critically endangered.

Wild axolotls must contend with loss of habitat due to drought; pollution, especially wastewater disposal; and human development. Other creatures eat the axolotls' eggs as well as their food. It is entirely possible that the next survey of Lake Xochimilco will find zero axolotls.

Or perhaps not. Scientists, conservationists, and others are figuring out how to cultivate and care for a rapidly dwindling population of wild axolotls: creating new natural habitats, pumping in clean water, and promoting responsible ecotourism. (For more on conservation efforts, see axiom 17 on page 62.) Because of genetic differences, axolotls bred in captivity cannot be released into the wild.

Repeatedly, conservationists have thought that axolotls had disappeared from their native habitat, only to rediscover them later. Somehow some have survived. Despite everything that's happened to them, they're holding on. Axolotls own their hard.

Owning your hard means coming to terms with the most difficult aspects of your life, whether past or present. It means not getting bowled over by troubles, felled by challenges, or overwhelmed by victimhood. It means getting help from a professional when such help is warranted. It means persevering rather than giving up, rejecting bitterness, getting some grit.

Widely considered to be the greatest basketball player of all time, Michael Jordan is grit personified. As he explained in a 1997 commercial for Nike: "I've missed more than 9,000 shots in my career. I've lost almost 300 games. Twenty-six times I've been trusted to take the game-winning shot and missed. I've failed over and over and over again in my life. And that is why I succeed." None of those failures would have been possible had Jordan not persevered through a potentially catastrophic situation: being cut from his high school varsity basketball team. He dealt with it, owning the hard rather than giving up, and eventually became His Airness. Giving up is the surest route to failure.

Katherine Johnson battled racism and sexism to become one of NASA's top mathematicians, helping send the first American astronauts to space. George Takei spent part of his childhood in Japanese internment camps, then went to (fictional) space as part of *Star Trek* and is now a leading LGBTQ+ and social justice advocate. Frida Kahlo took up painting at age 18 while recovering from a horrific bus accident that left her in horrible pain for the rest of her life. When bedridden, she'd use mirrors and a special easel.

Adopting an axolotl attitude requires you to combat the hard with effort. Instead of rolling over and letting the hard be in charge, you take control. Often, the first step to taking control entails acknowledging what's hard in the first place. Using as dispassionate a voice as possible, explain what's hard. Say it out loud, followed by this statement: "I can do hard things." Because you can.

FACT-CHECK YOUR FEELINGS

"We tell ourselves stories to live," wrote Joan Didion in 1979. Stories help us make sense of our experiences and our circumstances. We cast ourselves in the lead, and our minds create narratives that are bigger, brighter, and bolder than anything coming out of Hollywood. Too bad our stories—like the latest blockbuster—are often completely made up.

As humans, we tell a collective story about the innate superiority of our species. We cook with fire, we make art and weapons, we build multistory towers that stretch to the sky and software that reveals answers to any question in less time than it takes to blink.

We write songs like "We Are the Champions," then play them at top volume in the arena of our mind.

In 2003, scientists at the Human Genome Project announced that they had sequenced the human genome—a blueprint of what makes us human. It was a remarkable discovery, decades in the making, relying on international, open-source collaboration. Fifteen years later, scientists decoded the axolotl genome, some 32 billion base pairs compared to our (relatively puny) 3 billion base pairs.

Genome sequencing has led to some fascinating findings, including the fact that we share up to 60 percent of our genes with . . . wait for it . . . a banana. Yep, that phallic fruit that helps you poop is a distant cousin. Genetically, we're about 80 percent similar to a cow, 90 percent similar to a cat, and 96 percent similar to a chimpanzee. For the record, we share 99.6 percent of DNA with every other human on the planet.

How do those facts change our feelings? Maybe feelings of superiority start to evaporate, replaced with feelings of humility. Maybe you can finally stop comparing yourself to others. Maybe you're overcome by amusement or floored by the absurdity of knowing you are even a little similar to a banana.

Telling stories is part of what makes us human. Sometimes, though, our feelings lead us to create stories that may not be true at all. We might forget that feelings aren't facts—and that's when we might lose control, overreact instead of underreact (see axiom 7 on page 32), or get overwhelmed.

When your feelings become too much, distract yourself. Feeling all the feelings can be exhausting. Give yourself permission to put down the emotional burden for a while. That doesn't make you numb, nor does it make you incapable of empathy. It lets you recharge and figure out the right response. Divert yourself in these healthy, productive ways:

♡ Take a bath

♡ Write in a journal

♡ Text a friend

♡ Watch a favorite movie or show

♡ Go outside

♡ Drink a glass of water (see axiom 9 on page 38)

♡ Read a book

Imagine you're a mountain and your feelings are the weather. The fog rolls in, the fog rolls out. The sun shines, the sun sets. Sometimes it drizzles, sometimes it pours. The wind blows, then it blows harder. When you're in the weather, the weather seems all-encompassing. You can't see through the fog, nor can you escape the blinding sunshine. You tell yourself that the weather will never end. Yet, hard as it is to remember, the weather changes while the mountain perseveres. Distraction helps shift the weather and helps us differentiate between fact and fiction.

Similarly, talking to a professional can help you undertake an emotional overhaul or target a specific situation or feeling. Therapy can provide an umbrella, sunscreen, and myriad other tools to help you handle the weather and carry on with your life.

15

WATCH OUT FOR THOUGHT WORMS

Axolotls tend to be opportunistic eaters, swallowing whole whatever swims or gets sucked into their big mouths. They'll eat insects, crustaceans, tadpoles, and sometimes gravel, which is thought to aid with digestion. But they particularly like worms—bloodworms, earthworms, blackworms, mealworms, wax worms. For an axolotl, a wiggly worm is wonderful protein.

In 2020, researchers at Queen's University in Canada traced what they called "thought worms," or instances when the brain moves from one thought to another. They estimated that, on average, we think around 6,200 thoughts per day. Axolotls eat worms; we humans make them in our minds.

If you're anything like me, these thoughts range from the mundane (*I wonder what's for dinner*) to the random (*do animals have fingerprints?*) to the erroneous and illogical (*this Zoom meeting is going to kill me*). All of us fall prey to cognitive distortions—basically, faulty thinking that's generally negative.

Common cognitive distortions include catastrophizing (assuming the worst is always going to happen), overgeneralizing (drawing broad conclusions from very narrow evidence), mislabeling (using emotionally laden, sometimes damaging terminology), and personalizing (assuming everything is about you). Bad thoughts do damage, no doubt. Renowned for her quick wit, writer Dorothy Parker was also an alcoholic misanthrope who would say "What fresh hell can this be?" every time the doorbell rang. That kind of pessimism is insidious. Eventually it starts to act like a filter, distorting every experience with an unattractive, negative tint. Cognitive distortions can cause you to lose your sense of awe (see axiom 10 on page 41), optimism (see axiom 16 on page 59), and playfulness (see axiom 30 on page 101).

Luckily, the process works the other way as well. Hooray for the brain's plasticity! Positive thoughts have power, which is why people make vision boards and post to Pinterest. "Manifesting," or the belief that thinking something can make it happen, has become a huge phenomenon, with some 336 million hits on Google about how to do it.

One powerful technique for combating cognitive distortion is reframing. Case in point: Having a ton of work sucks. You can sit at your desk and think about how sucky it is to have so much to do. You can wallow in the suck, let the suck wash over you, pursue other avenues of suckitude, such as listing other things that suck. *This sucking will never end*, you think.

Sure, okay, that's one way to live. Alternatively, the next time things suck, try reframing and refocusing your energy. Having a ton of work also poses an opportunity. Maybe you'll get a chance to finally show off your shine to your boss. Or maybe the morass that is your in-box indicates that it might be time to offer your talents elsewhere. Either way, you now have a path through the suck that doesn't involve getting lost in it.

Other strategies, such as being mindful, help kill the inner critic (see axiom 8 on page 35) and encourage feelings of thankfulness. Slowing down (see axiom 31 on page 104) helps you fact-check your feelings (see axiom 14 on page 53) and break negative thought patterns. Ask yourself, *Why am I thinking this? Why am I feeling this?* Writing down your thoughts can help you find patterns and battle distortions.

Thought worms can be as squiggly as real worms. Just make sure your thoughts and thought worms serve you, nourish you, and help you grow.

16

KEEP GRINNING

You've probably heard of "Resting Bitch Face," or RBF, which makes a person look irritated or annoyed, regardless of how they're actually feeling. Among the most famous examples of celebrities with RBF are Queen Elizabeth and Kristen Stewart. Axolotls have Resting Grin Face, or RGF, making them appear constantly happy and completely blissed out.

Along with its plumy headgear, an axolotl's most distinguishing physical feature is its huge grin. Thanks to this countenance, an axolotl appears almost beatific as it swims around, casting an enigmatic smile on one and all.

This expression isn't about looking cute or exuding charisma—keeping its mouth open is an efficient hunting strategy. That is, an axolotl grins because it's the most effective means of catching whatever happens to be around, such as insect larvae and mollusks. What floats by gets pulled into that big mouth.

Look, if my favorite food magically appeared in my mouth without my having to buy or make it, I would beam all the time, too. And I might be better off, as smiling has been shown to confer many advantages, including the release of natural, feel-good hormones like serotonin and dopamine. Smiling reduces stress, strengthens your immune system, and boosts motivation.

A 2015 study from the University of London discovered what we know anecdotally to be true: when you smile, it feels as if the world is smiling back. In the study, smiling people rated other people's expressions as happier. Smiling puts good into the world and encourages good to be reflected back. Another UK study found that seeing a smile bestows the mental equivalent of consuming 2,000 chocolate bars.

When you're in need of a smile, listen to a comedy podcast. Follow funny people on social media. Look at old photos or texts on your phone. Grin at a friend or little kid. Give generously (see axiom 18 on page 65). Share good news. Sit up straight (there's a connection between good posture, confidence, and overall feelings of happiness). Smirk, chuckle, guffaw, bark with glee. No one ever exited this world wishing they'd laughed less in life.

Still, as anyone who's ever been told to smile knows, you can't necessarily force it. Some days are rotten, beyond the effect of good posture or a hilarious tweet. Even during the darkest hours, though, it's possible to cultivate hope and optimism. You might not feel like grinning, and that's fine. However, you can continue to believe that grins will, eventually, come again.

Having a generally rosy outlook confers crazy good stuff, physically and mentally, including increased problem-solving skills, decreased feelings of anxiety and fear, lower blood pressure, and a longer life span. A recent study found that, on average, being optimistic can lengthen a person's life by 11 to 15 percent.

As if that weren't amazing enough, the really super-awesome news is that optimism can be developed. Here are some ways you can train yourself to be more optimistic:

♡ Learn a new skill

♡ Imagine positive outcomes

♡ Celebrate your individual talents

♡ Keep a list of your proudest moments or wins

♡ Limit your news consumption

♡ Write down things you're grateful for

♡ Watch out for thought worms (see axiom 15 on page 56)

Whether you have RBF or RGF, you can learn to look on the bright side, find the silver lining, keep your chin up, and see the glass as half full of delicious lemonade—made from whatever lemons you've got kicking around—just waiting for you to take a big, refreshing sip.

17

FIND YOUR CREW

Without serious, sustained intervention, axolotls will go extinct very soon. Thankfully, teams of scientists, researchers, farmers, and activists are working together to keep axolotls safe and wild. Among the amphibian's biggest champions is Dr. Luis Zambrano, a professor at the Universidad Nacional Autónoma de México (National Autonomous University of Mexico) who has spent decades studying these creatures and witnessing their habitat destruction firsthand. As he told National Public Radio (NPR) in 2021: "[Axolotl extinction] is really, really concerning as a conservationist and as a Mexican because if we lose this species, we are losing part of our identity."

The Mexican government set aside the 530-acre Xochimilco Ecological Park and Plant Market in 1993 to help protect the axolotl habitat. However, despite this effort, not only has the area become increasingly polluted, it has also become something of a party zone, full of colorfully painted recreational boats known as *trajineras*.

More recently, a group of researchers led by Dr. Zambrano partnered with local farmers to develop the Chinampa Refuge Project. For thousands of years, farmers used *chinampas*, or floating islands, in Xochimilco to grow food. Reinvigorating this traditional system of farming creates healthy habitats for the axolotls as well as protecting them from their primary aquatic predators, tilapia and carp. Keeping the water pollution-free also aids the farmers and the ecosystem as a whole.

Like axolotls, people do best when surrounded by a caring crew. Decades of research have demonstrated the importance of relationships in people's lives. In fact, a groundbreaking meta-analysis of previously published research found that maintaining good relationships is on par with exercising and quitting smoking in terms of keeping you alive. Other studies have established a link between life span and socializing. Put another way: loneliness can kill you.

Drawing on research from sociologist Mark Granovetter, psychologists have determined that, when it comes to relationships, both quantity and quality matter. Granovetter developed the idea of "weak ties," or people with whom you have intermittent or occasional interactions. Examples of weak ties include someone you run into periodically at the yarn store, a fellow commuter who loves the Seattle Storm as much as you do, or a member of your synagogue or church. Think acquaintances, rather than bosom buddies, exchanging pleasantries rather than having heart-to-hearts. (Need help cultivating weak ties? See axiom 20 on page 71 for advice on upping your conversation game.) These casual acquaintances help us feel connected. You might have sensed what social science has shown: the greater the number of weak ties in our lives, the greater our feelings of empathy, contentment, and happiness.

As for our crew, we also need cheerleaders, or people with whom we have "strong ties." A cheerleader can be a friend, romantic partner, parent, coach, or mentor. You'll know if someone's a cheerleader if they can pass the hug test: Would your friend drop everything to give you a hug? That's "hug" in the actual sense of wrapped arms, but we also mean "hug" in a less literal sense. A cheerleader would Venmo you $100 to help you make rent, bring you soup when you're sick, and text you TikToks when you're sad. A cheerleader springs for the big bottle of champagne when you get the promotion. People with whom we have strong ties hang out in our corner and always have our back.

In time, a weak tie might grow stronger, and an acquaintance could turn into a best friend. The reverse holds as well. Such is life. Friendships and relationships change. What matters, though, is that we have a group of people to whom we are tied.

GIVE GENEROUSLY

In addition to regenerating their own body parts (see axiom 12 on page 47), axolotls can accept transplanted limbs and organs from other axolotls. A 1968 study in the eminent journal *Science* about transplanting heads includes this nightmarish fact: "The behavior of the transplants is independent of that of the host animals." Amazing and creepy! Mostly creepy!

Of course, the scientific literature doesn't detail how the axolotl heads divvied up thought responsibilities. Did one head focus on finding food and the other on watching for predators? Or did one head concentrate on processing sensations and the other on trying to remember the names of everyone they went to kindergarten with? Having a second head could be useful for storing info you need to know but don't necessarily need to access at all times, such as birthdays, state capitals, and when to use a semi-colon. It could be like a "go bag" you keep in the car, but crammed with entertaining facts and useful data rather than granola bars.

Regrettably, we're not quite there yet, so one head is what we've got for now. Setting aside the incredible applications for science and brainy multitasking, let's spare a thought for the axolotls who donated their heads in the service of scientific scholarship (see axiom 4 on page 23). And, in doing so, we can consider ways to be more giving in our own lives.

In December 2019, a new mural went up along the High Line, an elevated park in New York City. "The Baayfalls," by artist Jordan Casteel, portrays Fallou and Baaye Demba Sow, a Senegalese sister and brother, sitting in front of Fallou's hat stand in Harlem. Fallou's T-shirt reads, "I am not interested in competing with anyone. I hope we all make it."

Making art, then displaying art in a free park, where anyone can walk—that's generosity atop of generosity. You don't have to be an artist to take Casteel's message to heart. Can you look for ways to lift others in your life? Can you let go of competing? Can you be sympathetic and generous to yourself?

There are multiple ways to give generously: literally, as when you donate or make some kind of offering, or more figuratively, as in the message of Casteel's painting. You can pay for a stranger's coffee or let someone take the parking spot you had your eye on. You can proofread a friend's resume or give a book (such as this one!) a five-star review. Compliment someone's shoes, say thank you, forgive a transgression large or small. You can react to someone's ranting with empathy.

Studies have shown that people who give money away feel wealthier, regardless of the size of their back accounts. Activating and acting on our empathy appear to increase our sense of contentment. For a free and easy means of giving, try reciting a version of the loving-kindness meditation when walking in a crowded area. (Do it silently, so no one gets weirded out.)

May you be happy

May you be healthy

May you be peaceful

May you be protected

Giving generously means holding your tongue when you might otherwise make a critical comment. It means being the bigger person. It means picking up trash in your neighborhood or performing another act of service (see axiom 25 on page 86)— not for thanks or praise, but because things need to get done, and doing them spreads love, positivity, and kindness.

BROADEN YOUR MIND

The biological class Amphibia encompasses toads, newts, frogs, and more than 650 types of salamanders, including axolotls. Most amphibians begin life in the water, before maturing to live on land, a process known as *metamorphosis*. (Axolotls stay in the water their entire lives, a fact we dive into in axiom 30 on page 101.) We get the word *amphibian* from the Greek word *amphibios*, which means "living a double life."

Living a double life has justifiably negative connotations, among them duplicity and lying. When we say that someone lived a double life, we mean that they weren't honest—not the kind of person we want to be around or to emulate. Being an amphibian, however, has positive connotations, among them flexibility, broad-mindedness, and tolerance.

To be an amphibian is to take a little from column A, a little from column B. Amphibians avoid binaries; they disdain absolutes. They're not interested in black-and-white thinking, nor do they gravitate toward words such as "always" or "never." Instead, they comfortably inhabit a gray area.

In an otherwise unbelievably depressing 1936 essay, appropriately titled "The Crack-Up," F. Scott Fitzgerald perfectly encapsulated what we might call amphibian thinking: "The test of a first-rate intelligence is the ability to hold two opposed ideas in the mind at the same time, and still retain the ability to function." As an example, he says, people should be able to see things as hopeless but still want to improve them. Timeless advice, indeed.

Here's another example, with even more contemporary relevance: You can love someone but detest their politics. Yep, you can. Even better (and definitely harder), you can love someone, detest their politics, and listen to their point of view. As you listen, you can hold their point of view up to the light, checking for cracks or flaws, as you would a diamond. Views are precious to those who hold them, so treat opposing views with respect. Then break out the metaphorical loupe, pop it into your eye like a jeweler, and check for holes or fallacies in their thinking, as well as your own. Ultimately, you don't have to change your mind; you should, though, strive to broaden it.

Sometimes people joke about living in bubbles. There's nothing funny about surrounding yourself with people who have the exact same opinions or outlooks. How much better off we are when we spend time with people who aren't the same as us. That's how we grow. Furthermore, getting a multiplicity of views helps ensure viable solutions to complicated problems.

If we could all take a step toward listening, and a step away from knee-jerk reactions, we might be able to learn something. We might be able to find common ground, as opposed to automatically dismissing a person or point of view.

It's up to you to determine the line at which someone or something moves from tolerable, if erroneous, to toxic. Make sure to look at the line. It's easy to fall into the default attitude of treating someone else's beliefs like cruddy rhinestones and scorning them without a second thought.

Granted, you don't need to listen to discriminatory talk to know that it's flat-out wrong. Otherwise, engage in dialogue. Be respectful. Entertain counterarguments. Consider the other side. Get gray. Be amphibian! You might still find your view to be the right one—bully for you! Remember that sharing your views only with those with whom you already agree gets you nothing but nods or likes. It won't grow your brain, it won't expand your world view, and it doesn't help nurture a first-rate intelligence.

UP YOUR CONVERSATION GAME

Some axolotl pet parents report that their creatures recognize them and will swim over to an outstretched hand for a nuzzle or pat. More likely, the axolotl associates the vibrations with food and zooms over to see what treats might be in store. Sorry, people.

With one another, axolotls communicate using chemical and visual signals, most often when mating. The strongest form of axolotl communication occurs at the cellular level: after a wound, an axolotl's cells interact, grouping into what's called a *blastema*. Cells inside a blastema "de-differentiate," or shed their identity, and become similar to stem cells, thus enabling regrowth—exactly how this works is still a bit TBD for scientists (see axiom 12 on page 47 for a fuller discussion of an axolotl's regenerative talents). Okay, I'm not going to go on and on here about how conversation is becoming a lost art. (But it kinda is.) I'm not going to drone on about the evils of being inseparable from our smartphones. (I like being able to Google "theme song Family Ties guitar" without leaving my couch as much as the next person.) So I'll say this instead: There will be times in life when you're forced to speak with someone you don't know. And when that moment comes, you'll be grateful if you can communicate like an axolotl.

Depending on where you fall on the introvert-extrovert spectrum, strangers might be friends you haven't met yet. Or, if you're more introverted, small talk might give you hives and make you want to hide under the covers. Either way, it helps to have a list of questions at your disposal. Sure, you can always default to asking how people know the bride(s) or groom(s) at a wedding, or you can marvel at how sunny/rainy/windy/cold it is. Wow, weather! The truth is that cultivating good conversation takes work beyond the humdrum basics. And the secret is to ask open-ended questions (that is, questions that can't be answered with a "yes" or "no"). Questions like these encourage conversation, a back-and-forth, a verbal give-and-take. Here are some possibilities to keep in your pocket:

♡ What was the first concert you went to?

♡ What hobby did you take up during the pandemic? Did it stick?

- ♡ Which actor would you want to play you in a movie of your life?
- ♡ As a child, what was your dream job?
- ♡ What has been your biggest fashion fail? *Note:* This one works particularly well if you can first compliment something the person is wearing.
- ♡ What's your secret talent? What are you better at than anyone else?
- ♡ What's your favorite photo on your phone?
- ♡ What's the best food you've ever eaten?

The best conversation starters take you past pleasantries. They often reveal interesting information, which could lead to commonalities: "Wait, you wanted to be a professional wrestler? Me, too! What was your favorite move?" Soon enough you'll be chatting away.

Naturally, when you ask a question, you need to be prepared to answer it yourself. For instance, my dream job as a child was being an artist and living in a van in Europe. I could have been an OG on the #vanlife, but, alas, my life went in a different direction, one that involved running water and a house that can't roll away. Having a hobby (axiom 24 on page 83) and picking a cause (axiom 25 on page 86) mean you'll always have fun facts and titillating tidbits to share.

21

KEEP CHOOSING YOUR PARTNER

Some animals mate for life. Axolotls are not those animals.

Instead, axolotls are more opportunistic. When mating time rolls around, axolotls engage in what scientists have described as a "waltz," which involves the two salamanders prodding one another's cloacae (a *cloaca* is the single orifice used for digestive, urinary, and reproductive functions in many animals). Once the male has released his sperm—after about 30 seconds of hearty gesticulating with his tail—the female and the male have no further interaction. After the female has laid 300 to 1,000 eggs, usually on rocks or plants, she skedaddles. Two weeks later, the eggs hatch.

Sadly, all of us probably know a human family that bears some resemblance to the aforementioned axolotl version. Um, at the risk of stating the obvious: don't be that family.

Here's another obvious sentiment that might nevertheless warrant repeating: you don't need a partner. If you're not in a relationship for whatever reason, choose yourself. Or choose a partner, temporary or otherwise, or multiple partners. You do you (and/or others) in whatever ways are healthy, safe, consensual, and pleasurable for everyone involved.

If you are in a relationship, and you want to stay in that relationship, choose your partner. Then keep choosing that same partner. Umpteenth time after umpteenth time—even when your partner says "upteenth," rather than "umpteenth." At some point in any relationship, the bloom comes off the rose. You discover that your partner believes in aliens, or was only pretending to like Frisbee golf as much as you do. Now you have a choice. You can grab your partner's hand and scan the night sky, searching for UFOs, or you can say "so long." Rest assured that, if you decide to stay, you will be presented with many more opportunities to choose. Big choices, little choices—life-shattering, heartbreaking choices. Being in a relationship entails discovering things about the other person, and about yourself, that you might not wish to know. The question is, once you know them, what do you want to do?

College sweethearts Samuel L. Jackson and LaTanya Richardson Jackson attribute their multidecade marriage to a decision "to stick together no matter what." As the actors explained to *People* in 2022, this pact saw them through professional rejection, addiction, and emotional abandonment—not easy things to overcome or forgive. It also saw them through career accomplishments as well as the highs and lows of raising a daughter. They stayed together through it all.

To be clear: no one is knocking anyone for splitting up or getting divorced. What the Jacksons contended with might be deal-breaking for others. And that's the point: the Jacksons chose to stay together, then kept choosing. They might have made different choices, then coped with or celebrated the consequences. That's life! It's the act of choosing that counts.

If you're choosing to stay, then channel the Jacksons and keep choosing. Unfortunately, unless we're extremely careful, the person who tends to receive the biggest dose of our anger/resentment/sadness/[insert other negative emotion] is the person with whom we're spending the most time, especially our partner. Try to choose *not* to do that.

Actively choosing your partner, whether you've been together for a little while or since the first Bush administration, entails asking your partner to do the same for you. Share your needs (see axiom 6 on page 29). Develop special rituals (see axiom 26 on page 89). Treat each other like the miracles you are (see axiom 1 on page 14). Give care, take care, and patch cracks quickly lest they turn into irreparable breaks. Say yes and yes and, a thousand times, yes.

22

SET BOUNDARIES

Axolotls lack armor, fur, feathers, scales, light sabers, venom, Kevlar, or other defense mechanisms. As amphibians, they do have a protective layer of mucus, FWIW, but are otherwise very, very bare. Some axolotls are even barer: while reduced pigmentation could be problematic in the wild, where axolotls try to blend in with vegetation, leucistic axolotls have become popular pets, because their skin is almost translucent. You can see their skeletons.

That skeleton includes a backbone. Axolotls are vertebrates, a group of animals with a backbone. Vertebrates make up just 3 percent of all the known animals in the world; the other 97 percent are invertebrates, such as sea stars and spiders.

Like an axolotl, we humans have a backbone. We, too, lack cool natural defense mechanisms, such as the ability to make flesh-rotting venom (like a slow loris) or a putrid glue out of vomit (like a subarctic seabird). Boundaries are a form of armor, a way of protecting ourselves, fostering our independence, and promoting our well-being.

This idea has implications on two fronts: physical and mental. Let's talk physical first. Set your boundaries. End of story. If someone crosses those boundaries without asking for and receiving your BLC (Big Loud Consent), get yourself out of the situation ASAP. That is 100 percent nonnegotiable. Your body, your boundaries. Same goes for asking for consent. Ask, then wait to hear whether ye shall receive.

For examples of erotic consent, check out contemporary romance novels, such as *One Last Stop* by Casey McQuiston, a time-traveling rom-com that somehow makes even romping on the New York City subway sexy. McQuiston repeatedly connects consent with her protagonist's burgeoning understanding of her sexuality. Consent is a form of empathy between the two lovers.

But always putting others first can complicate the setting of mental boundaries. Some people have trouble saying no, and thus they're the ones fixing the printer while everyone else is at happy hour. An axolotl's grin belies its feistiness. Axolotls have claws and teeth, and will use them if provoked (see axiom 7 on page 32). We're not recommending that you bite anyone (unless, you know, everyone's down with that). We are, however, recommending that you find your feistiness when it comes to boundaries.

It's okay to hop off the group text. Skip Thanksgiving, if that's what you need to do to avoid damaging drama or toxic relationships. Ignore that 11 p.m. work email. It's fine to politely decline an invitation to your best friend's cousin's first grader's karaoke party. Learning to say no is a necessary art. If, on the other hand, hearing a bunch of seven-year-olds belt out "We Don't Talk about Bruno" floats your boat, by all means go and enjoy yourself.

Carve out space in your schedule to write that script or earn your degree in interior design (see axiom 29 on page 98 for more advice about how to organize your life). Tell people about your "me time," then stick to that schedule. If you don't respect your own boundaries, others won't either.

Much of life is figuring out your needs (see axiom 6 on page 29). What do you need to be happy, healthy, stay motivated, keep going? Once you've figured out your needs, you can begin to set boundaries and, just as important, communicate them to others. Calmly explain but do not make excuses for your boundaries. No apologies, no exceptions.

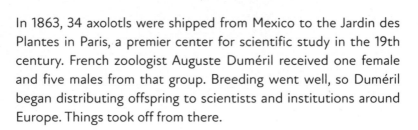

BLOOM WHERE YOU'RE PLANTED

In 1863, 34 axolotls were shipped from Mexico to the Jardin des Plantes in Paris, a premier center for scientific study in the 19th century. French zoologist Auguste Duméril received one female and five males from that group. Breeding went well, so Duméril began distributing offspring to scientists and institutions around Europe. Things took off from there.

Since then, axolotls have become among the most successful animals in laboratory settings in history (see axiom 4 on page 23 to hear about their contributions to science). *Smithsonian* magazine calls them "basically the white mice of amphibians." Today, descendants of Duméril's group can be found at the University of

Kentucky, home to what is perhaps the world's most important axolotl stock center, having traveled over the years from Paris to Kraków (Poland) to Buffalo (New York) to Bloomington (Indiana) to Lexington (Kentucky).

The axolotl offers a master class in blooming where you're planted. We often find ourselves in less-than-ideal circumstances, in large and small ways. We get rejected by our dream school and wind up at our third-choice college. We take an internship that turns out to be quite different from what we expected, or we get roped into a family business and never leave our hometown.

Reality frequently doesn't meet our expectations, whether that's because those expectations were wildly off base or because things actually do sort of stink. That leaves us with a choice: to get out, or to get cracking.

This axiom never applies to situations that are damaging or dangerous. In those instances, you want to trust your instincts. Immediately remove yourself from anything that could prove mentally or physically harmful. There will be no blooming, and there is no choice.

But a situation that's bleh or meh? Mildly irritating and annoying? B minus rather than A plus? Consider toughing it out and making the best of it. Doing so might reveal a strength or an interest you never knew you had.

Take Mary Barra, who began her career with General Motors on the assembly line, inspecting the fit between fenders and hoods. She was 18. Today, she serves as the company's chair and CEO. In her long career, she's worked in GM's Human Resources department, managed an assembly plant, and overseen engineering and product development. Pretty much the only time she's spent away from the company was to earn an MBA from Stanford.

Sometimes blooming where you're planted means making the best of whatever situation you're in, even as you're setting your sights on something bigger. As a child, Misty Copeland would use the balcony outside of the motel where she lived with her single mom and five siblings as a barre. She slept on the floor. In 2015, she became the first Black female principal dancer in the history of the prestigious American Ballet Theatre.

Go ahead and accept the crappy assignment from your boss. Better yet, raise your hand for the unfun assignment nobody wants and give it your all. When the time comes to move on, you'll have a reputation as a self-starter. Put up new curtains in your crummy rental apartment where the kitchen is carpeted and the doorbell rings whenever you turn on the lights in the living room. When the time comes to move out, you'll have a funny story to tell at dinner parties. Bloom where you're planted.

Take a few minutes to be grateful for wherever you are at this particular moment, for whatever you can learn or grow from. Don't lose sight of the fact that circumstances will change. They always do.

HAVE A HOBBY

Having a hobby has fallen out of favor. It feels silly, like something that should be left behind as one transitions out of childhood. In our age of uber-productivity and perfectionism, it feels pointless. People say they're too busy to do anything besides work or raise a family, then spend six hours inhaling social media (yep, that's me—guilty as charged).

I have a friend who collects regional drinks like maple soda and birch beer wherever he goes. Another friend loves board games. Nail art, canning, kayaking, Viking-era cosplay, taking care of axolotls—there's no end to what you might adopt as a hobby. Some hobbies are solitary; some foster socializing. Every single one gives you fun facts to share at parties. The goal of having a hobby, first and foremost, is to have fun.

White House adviser Tim Wu has attributed our lack of hobbies to a fear of failure. Given our culture's relentless pursuit of perfection, being bad at something is no longer acceptable. It's not enough to hike for an hour; we must complete the Appalachian Trail. It's not enough to make a wreath to hang on your door; you must open an Etsy shop and start selling, or chronicle your efforts on a blog full of printables.

Along with not wanting to be bad at something, we have trouble admitting to leisure time. Instead, we complain (or brag) about how busy we are—an attitude even Roman emperor Marcus Aurelius laments in *Meditations*, his book of Stoic self-help and advice written in the second century. Saying you have time for a hobby is (still) frowned upon.

Everyone has to make a living, and side hustles can be awesome. But having a hobby offers an opportunity to create, explore, or experience without a specific goal. Hobbies let you enjoy your free time, giving you a break from work and chores. They let you play (see why play matters in axiom 30 on page 101). You don't have to specialize or become an expert; you don't have to sell or document what you make. Spending an afternoon filling in a coloring book, building a robot, surfing, making miniature furniture, or exploring your neighborhood just for kicks is absolutely okay.

If you're looking for a hobby related to axolotls, consider herpetology, the study of amphibians and reptiles. People who enjoy herpetology are known as *herpers*. A herper might wish to adopt an axolotl as a pet (see Be an Axolotl [Pet] Parent on page 111) or create a *stumpery*. First developed in Victorian England, this style of garden relies on felled trees, roots, and stumps. Stumperies aren't only artful; as they decay, tree parts serve as homes for various animals, including some species of salamander (depending on where you live).

Another way to attract reptiles and salamanders to your yard is to plant native flora. Not mowing your lawn as often, or setting the blade on a higher setting, also helps create a happy environment for lizards, toads, frogs, and snakes.

Herper, stumpery—in addition to making you a more interesting, engaged person, having a hobby gives you an entirely new vocabulary. It makes you more connected—online or IRL—as you find people who similarly wish to bring salamanders to their backyards, throw axes, Photoshop pets onto movie posters, or read tarot cards.

A hobby can also save your life. In February 2022, when an 80-year-old woman neglected to text her daughter with an update about Wordle, an online word game, the younger woman got worried. She called the authorities, who discovered a home invasion in progress. What's a five-letter word for *un-freaking-believable*?

25

PICK A CAUSE

Much like having a hobby (see axiom 24 on page 83), having a cause makes you a more engaged, more interesting person. Consider the difference between hobbies and causes this way: A hobby is something you do, an activity like sketching or playing Dungeons & Dragons. A cause is something you believe in and advocate for, such as buying local or social justice. Your hobby can be connected to your cause, such as being an axolotl pet parent (see Be an Axolotl [Pet] Parent on page 111) and being involved in wildlife conservation, or it can be separate.

The world has problems that need fixing, for sure, and picking a cause allows you to be a problem-solver, as opposed to a problem-dweller or problem-ignorer. Doomscrolling leads to obsessing, which leads to feeling overwhelmed and incapacitated. Burying your head in the sand and ignoring genuine issues lead to indifference and apathy. Ignorance is decidedly not bliss.

Focusing on a single cause helps you strike a balance between dwelling and ignoring. Whereas having multiple causes might feel overwhelming, one cause lets you hone in, educate yourself, and make an actual difference. It gives you an outlet and means for making the world a better place while enabling you to resist the urge to curl up into a ball every time you read the newspaper.

Start by digging into whatever interests you. Go down a Reddit rabbit hole focused on an issue that concerns you. Check out Charity Navigator to see how different nonprofits use donations. Sign up for emails or newsletters; create a fundraiser on social media for your birthday.

Volunteering has been shown to reduce anxiety and increase well-being, among other positives. Donate your talents and your time (see axiom 18 on page 65 for more advice on giving generously). Proselytize (when appropriate) so that others learn about why your cause matters and why you care about it. Be passionate but not alienating, knowledgeable but not fanatical. Having a cause means you'll never lack for conversation (see axiom 20 on page 71 for more tips on talking).

Be a good citizen of your part of the world, wherever you may be. When you see trash on your street or local park, pick it up. Participate in a citizen science project to monitor wildlife in your community, such as HerpMapper (for reptiles and amphibians), FrogWatch USA, or the Great Backyard Bird Count. Help kids through DonorsChoose, a website founded in 2000 by Bronx teacher Charles Best to encourage people to learn about and donate to classroom projects. Nowadays DonorsChoose is available at thousands of public schools in the United States. Find one near you, and send art supplies, books, or hand sanitizer.

Be a good citizen of the world, because it's the only one we've got (so far). Named for primatologist Jane Goodall, Trees for Jane seeks to reforest and regreen the earth, as well as protect what's already growing. Conservation International looks for ways to restore ecosystems, primarily in the Americas. Environmental issues disproportionately impact low-income communities and communities of color. Connect with organizations such as We ACT for Environmental Justice and Indigenous Environmental Network to learn more.

If ever you lose heart and begin to question the effectiveness of your efforts, remember this quote, attributed to cultural anthropologist Margaret Mead: "Never doubt that a small group of committed citizens can change the world. Indeed, that is all that ever has."

26

RELY ON RITUALS

Animals rely on rituals to navigate a complicated world. As behavioral ecologist Caitlin O'Connell points out in *Wild Rituals*, repeated, deliberate actions help animals bond with their communities, make decisions, and forecast the future. Red deer roar, rhinos cross horns, giraffes entwine necks, gorillas cuddle. Axolotls perform a wiggly dance before mating that some scientists have likened to waltzing (see axiom 21 on page 74 for more info). Each of these behaviors conveys information and emotion.

That holds true for us as well. We repeat actions collectively or individually, to foster connections, decrease anxiety, and send signals. Before many Hindu, Sikh, or Muslim weddings, for instance, the wedding party and guests might participate in a Mehndi ceremony, in which henna designs are applied to feet and hands. Along with ornamenting and beautifying, the henna, or Mehndi, acts as a calming coolant that helps alleviate nerves. The party itself features dancing, socializing, and food, and kicks off the next day's nuptials.

Religious ceremonies are full of rituals, but we can develop our own rituals to decrease uncertainty and give our brains a shortcut. O'Connell defines *ritual* as "a specific act or series of acts that are performed in a precise manner and repeated often." Taking a Pilates class every Wednesday, or making a to-do list every day before you shut down your computer, provides some structure. Stopping at a particular pizza place on the way from the airport whenever you visit your hometown eases you into a visit with your family. You know what's coming next. A ritual generates positive associations, much as a bath-book-bed routine helps sleep train babies.

Bespoke rituals can create order. Putting on a work uniform— whether it's a suit and tie, comfy leggings, or a set of scrubs—tells your brain that it's time to get down to business. A bassoonist might always begin by playing scales in a certain way, while a carpenter might start a job by sharpening a few pencils. Like donning work clothes, these actions signal a transition, from nonwork mode to work mode.

Speaking of work, our rituals are a great way to encourage us to avoid procrastination and cultivate *sitzfleisch*. This German word technically means "sitting meat," but it's taken on a new meaning in the work world. *Sitzfleisch* is how stuff gets done, through work or practice. Romance novelist Nora Roberts attributes her jaw-dropping productivity—more than 220 novels (and counting) over her long career—to sitting meat, only she puts it much more colorfully: "ass in the chair." As you might have noticed, Roberts doesn't specify a kind of chair, a time of day, or a type of desk. She sits, she writes. You can't become the next Doja Cat without spending serious time in the studio. Having a ritual, such as making a cup of tea or lighting a candle, can get you into your chair, metaphorically speaking. It can trick your brain into working.

Becoming overly reliant on a routine or ritual, however, can create anxiety and impede our flow. Always beginning a project by dumping your data into a spreadsheet can kick-start your process, but painstakingly selecting different fonts for each row can be a form of procrastinating—a particularly dangerous one, at that, for it can feel as if you're accomplishing something and moving forward. Overreliance on rituals can be a sign of a bigger issue, from burnout to depression. If you ever start to sense a profound change in your feelings or your behavior, make an appointment to speak with your doctor.

27

TAKE CARE OF YOUR SPACE

Whether in the wild, the lab, or a home aquarium, axolotls rely on us to take care of their space. We have a responsibility to these creatures, considering the outsize role humans play in the climate crisis generally and the destruction of the axolotl environment specifically (learn more about axolotl conservation efforts in axiom 17 on page 62).

In Lake Xochimilco, the only native axolotl habitat left on earth, axolotls spend most of their time hanging out in plants or along the lake's muddy bottom. In tanks, axolotls need cool, clean water. They like stillness and find rapidly moving or circulating water stressful.

"Do not stress out the axolotls" is pretty good advice. So is "understand your impact on the planet." You can begin by using an online tool to calculate your carbon footprint, or the amount of greenhouse gases produced as you go about your daily life. You'll be asked to estimate such things as how much money you spend on shoes, what you recycle, and how often you drive.

Emissions data in hand, you can look for ways to shrink your footprint. For example, according to the Meatless Monday campaign, swapping a plant-based option for a burger at a single meal can save the equivalent of the energy needed to power a smartphone for six months, as well as 10 bathtubs of water. Never underestimate the effect of a small gesture.

If you're inspired to do more, do more! Picking a cause (see axiom 25 on page 86) helps combat apathy and is fundamental to leading an axolotl life. Perhaps your cause is environmental in nature. If you're assiduous about recycling, try composting. Shop vintage, and donate your clothes rather than chucking them in the trash (about 85 percent of old clothes wind up in landfills). Wash your clothes in cold water, which uses less energy than hot water. Take public transportation, walk, or ride a bike.

Along with our global caretaking responsibility comes an individual responsibility. In other words, we have to take care of our own space, too. As Gretchen Rubin posits in *Outer Order, Inner Calm*, being in control of our stuff can help us gain control over our lives. Sadly, that box by the door won't fill itself with knickknacks you hate, lift itself into the car, and drive itself over to Goodwill. Unfortunately, that toothpaste glob on the counter won't unglob itself, no matter how much time you give it. You've got to get involved.

Set aside a few minutes each day to tidy and clean. It is far, far easier to do a little bit of something every day than to wait to do a massive decluttering or deep cleaning. Just thinking about spending your whole weekend cleaning is probably enough to send you back to bed on a Saturday. Aim for baby steps: keep microfiber cloths in the bathroom, and give your counter a periodic wipe. Clean up spills when they happen. Put away your clothes as soon as you take them off or pull them out of the dryer. Make your bed.

As with taking care of the planet, if you're inspired to do more, do more! Break out the baking soda and vinegar, and get to scrubbing. Refold your socks and T-shirts into space-saving shapes; color-code your closet by season. Give away things you're keeping out of obligation or sentimentality. Caring for your space can absolutely be a way of caring for yourself—or it can be just a thing you have to do before you get to do whatever it is you truly want it to do. Either way, it's important to take time to tidy.

28

ADORE THE BORING

Axolotls do not lead what anyone would call an exciting life. They mature, they mate, they swim, they eat, they sleep. Largely solitary in the wild, they camouflage themselves in vegetation or mud. With the exception of their marvelous regenerative powers and occasional cannibalism (see axiom 7 on page 32 and axiom 12 on page 47), their day-to-day is pretty unremarkable.

Other animals arguably lead more exciting lives. Suriname toads give birth through womb pockets in their back. (Intrigued? Feel free to Google, but don't say I didn't warn you.) The tiny arctic tern has one of the longest migrations of any animal: more than 25,000 miles, a zigzagging annual route from pole to pole, with stops in North America, Africa, and Australia. Komodo dragons have awesome appetites, eating up to 80 percent of their body weight in a single meal, while some dung beetles are Superman-style strong, maneuvering balls of poo more than 1,000 times their body weight.

You could say that the same goes for humans. While some of us seemingly spend our days mucking around in the mud, feeling as if we're just punching life's time card, others jet around the globe, racking up more frequent-flier miles than an arctic tern and documenting the best of the best on social media. Therein lies an important point: the highlights get documented, discussed, boasted about, and remembered. The truth is that every life has its share of boredom as well as highlights.

"I have measured out my life with coffee spoons," laments the speaker of "The Love Song of J. Alfred Prufrock," a poem T. S. Eliot wrote when he was only 26. If we're lucky enough to live a long time, we'll have plenty of coffee spoons to look forward to. That's to say nothing of all the made and unmade beds, loads of laundry, time spent on hold, and thousands of other mundane things we have to deal with.

Researchers have concluded that each of us has a base level of happiness. So, after an initial surge of joy (winning the lottery!) or surge of pain (losing a loved one), we eventually settle back to wherever we were before the very positive or negative event. Otherwise known as "hedonic adaptation," we tend to adjust to new circumstances and return to our usual emotional programming rather quickly.

Hedonic adaptation is the reason why your 50th trip to Disneyland is less fun than your first. It's why you might start to take your partner for granted, and why you sometimes look back on an experience that seemed terrible at the time and think "that wasn't so bad."

When the grind really feels like a grind, we can nudge our happiness threshold by turning routine into ritual (for more on rituals, see axiom 26 on page 89) and finding some joy every day. Just as important, these moments of joy should be varied. Take a new route to work on Monday, noticing the cherry blossoms on your way. Wear your favorite sweater on Tuesday, try a new café on Wednesday, call your best friend on Thursday. Set your computer password to something rad or randy.

Seize small, simple pleasures! Don't discount them simply because they're small. Instead, embrace them because they are always available to you. Schedule them if you have to, as anticipation tends to heighten the pleasure of experiences. Keep in mind that periods of boredom allow us to recharge and reset.

If we spend too much time scanning the horizon, we miss the wonders beneath our feet. When we're always chasing the grand or the new, we can't focus on the now, and now is all there is.

29

ORGANIZE YOUR LIFE

Located in southwestern Montana, the Axolotl Lakes recreation area consists of 10 little lakes and 400-odd acres of land. You can hike, camp, bird-watch, picnic, fish, and catch the creatures that give the area its name. Trouble is, you'll be bagging *Ambystoma mavortium.*

It was Aristotle who first proposed a classification system for animals: those with blood and those without. Roughly 2,000 years later, Swedish botanist Carl Linnaeus crystallized the modern method of organizing organisms known as "binomial nomenclature," in which plants and animals are given a generic name (genus) and a specific name (species). Animals usually have a common name as well.

According to scientific classification, axolotls are *Ambystoma mexicanum*. (For more information on axolotl nomenclature, see axiom 2 on page 17.) The so-called axolotls of Montana are barred tiger salamanders, closely related to but technically different from the axolotls of central Mexico.

My high school history teacher—let's call her Mrs. G.—would begin and end every class the same way: by shouting, "Organize your life." Her catchphrase appeared on the blackboard, on our papers about the Revolutionary War and the Treaty of Versailles, and whenever someone fumbled an answer to a question.

Calling the Montanan amphibians "axolotls" is, to some degree, a failure of organization. No offense to the Bureau of Land Management, which oversees the area, but what we have here might be termed a lack of attention to detail.

While it feels weird to lump Mrs. G. in with Aristotle and Linnaeus, they were all correct that organization matters. We get only so many hours in the day; we have only so much energy; our attention spans are only so long. Maintaining a schedule—otherwise known as "organizing your life"—helps us make the most of our time.

To organize your life, start by doing a "time audit." Keep a record of what you do and when you do it for a few days. No cheating, no judgments. After a week or so, you'll have a sense of your typical routine. Then you can begin figuring out what's working for you and what isn't. Are you spending your days in ways that match your values? In ways that strengthen your relationships, better your brain, and enhance your life?

If you need to reorganize, think in terms of 90-minute blocks. A seminal study of violinists, undertaken in 1993 by psychologist K. Anders Ericsson, discovered that the most elite group practiced for intense bursts (around 90 minutes at a time), took regular breaks and naps, and usually capped their practice at 4½ hours a day. At least one practice session occurred in the morning. Although Ericsson's sample size was small, his team's findings have been repeated in similar studies of other top musicians, athletes, and executives.

Extrapolate from Ericsson's study, and schedule a hard task first thing in the morning, when you're at your freshest. Own your hard (see axiom 13 on page 50) and get it done. Then make time for play (see axiom 30 on page 101). Schedule breaks. Take a few hours to read *How to Do Nothing,* the bestseller by Jenny Odell, and consider what productivity means to you. Adjust your schedule and commitments accordingly.

There will always be more work, more asks, more requests, more demands on your attention, your energy, your money, your very self, an endless loop of hassles. "I just don't fuck with chaos," actor Natasha Lyonne told *The New Yorker* in 2022. In other words, organize your life!

30

STAY YOUNG

One reason axolotls are so cute is that they look like supersized tadpoles. Axolotls are neotenic, which means they keep juvenile (larval) characteristics into adulthood. Unlike other salamanders, axolotls don't metamorphose. Instead, they retain their feathery rami (see axiom 5 on page 26 for more info about axolotl headgear) as well as their dorsal fin and remain in the water for their entire lives, even as they mature and reproduce. Axolotls look young because, technically, they are young, regardless of age. *National Geographic* refers to them as "forever-babies."

It's possible that the cause of axolotl neoteny is that they didn't need to get onto land when they first evolved 10,000 years ago. They were the top predators in their natural habitat. In that relatively unchanging, peaceful environment, and without significant aquatic stressors, axolotls could safely stay in the water from birth through death, thus conserving the energy required for metamorphosis.

Today, unfortunately, axolotls are beset by a number of stressors, including human encroachment (as Mexico City expands) and pollution. In the 1970s, African tilapia and common carp were introduced to help feed the human population. The non-native fish have become invasive species, gobbling axolotl eggs and competing with adult axolotls for food. (See axiom 17 on page 62 for more info about conservation efforts.)

As humans grow up, we're encouraged to shed various childhood attributes. Our loveys get donated to Goodwill; our imaginary friends float away. Many of us trade crayons for calculus, stop stomping through puddles and put on sensible shoes, cease saying the alphabet backward or collecting knock-knock jokes. We stop being silly and we stop playing.

For kids, play is serious work. Through play, kids develop social skills, imagination, confidence, and other competencies. Play helps children figure out who they are in the world. They use that knowledge to get better at, and do more of, what they're good at—and, as a consequence, they grow up and forget how to play.

Yet, playing conveys big benefits for adults, including decreasing stress and promoting positive coping strategies. Play provides a welcome distraction when things get tough and can lead to creative solutions. Acting playful together can improve relationships. Scientists have found that play can alter our brains for the better. Last but not least, play connects us to who we once were, offering a bridge from our adult self to our child self. For both children and adults, play can be a direct conduit to joy.

After a certain age, though, straight-up play can be uncomfortable. Whereas kids can lose themselves in play, adults often feel self-conscious and awkward. Figuring out what kind of play you gravitate toward can help lessen the discomfort. A 2017 study looked at four personality traits associated with playfulness:

- ♡ Whimsical (enjoys weird or odd things in everyday life)
- ♡ Lighthearted (relishes improvisation and spontaneity)
- ♡ Intellectual (prefers brainwork, such as riddles and wordplay)
- ♡ Other-directed (likes jokes and spirited social exchanges)

Think about which trait you most identify with, then find some activities that fit. A person whose play style tends toward whimsical might enjoy finding shapes in the clouds, while a person who likes to make people laugh might practice improvisations. Obviously some people might like play that fits into multiple categories, such as making up funny songs with friends about the clouds they see.

Above all, playing shouldn't be a source of stress. If it feels like fun, then you're 100 percent doing it right.

31

SLOW DOWN

To rationalize skipping school and having the most epic hooky day in history, as documented in the 1986 movie *Ferris Bueller's Day Off*, Ferris turns to the camera and declares, "Life moves pretty fast. If you don't stop and look around once in a while, you could miss it."

Most of the time, axolotls adopt a Bueller-like attitude. During the day, they hide out in plants or murky water, watching the world go by with their unblinking eyes. Then, as night falls, they begin hunting (learn more in axiom 16 on page 59). When necessary, they can move as quickly as a remarkable 10 miles per hour, which is roughly three times faster than the average human walks. Generally, though, moving that fast isn't necessary.

"How we do anything is how we do everything," goes the saying. Slowing down allows us to be careful and encourages us to be conscientious. Researchers at the University of Minnesota have found that conscientiousness is among the best predictors of success and happiness. Being conscientious encompasses a variety of characteristics, including self-control, organization, persistence, discipline, and concentration.

The following are some ways you can slow down, cultivate conscientiousness, and be more axolotl:

♡ Walking (seeing the world at foot speed has the additional advantage of helping us reduce our environmental impact, as discussed in axiom 27 on page 92)

♡ Taking a breath (see axiom 5 on page 26)

♡ Underreacting (see axiom 7 on page 32)

♡ Having a hobby (see axiom 24 on page 83)

♡ Cultivating special rituals (see axiom 26 on page 89)

♡ Drinking a glass of water (see axiom 9 on page 38)

♡ Organizing your life (see axiom 29 on page 98)

In fact, going slow is probably the ultimate axolotl axiom. Working slowly means working carefully, which leads to fewer mistakes and less stress. Slow resistance training has been shown to help increase muscle strength, and low-impact exercise often offers many of the same gains as high-impact exercise. Eating slowly helps you eat with all five senses and savor your meals. Living slowly means making intentional choices, rather than rushing about or defaulting into situations. With slowness come patience, calmness, mindfulness, and deeper relationships.

Slowing down isn't sexy, sparkly, or speedy. It means being more like the turtle than the hare, more like snail mail than email.

When you slow down, you're able to take your own measure. You'll have the chance to ask yourself whether you really want to move to Los Angeles, eat that slice of cherry pie, buy the cabin, take that job, go to the club, have that argument, do another rep. Simply asking yourself to stop and think helps you build strength and confidence, because you'll know that you've weighed your options and thought through the outcomes. And you'll get the benefit of understanding yourself, which is never a bad thing.

Note that slowing down doesn't mean letting go of your goals. Just the opposite. By being intentional and deliberate, you can concentrate on what you want, how you can get it, and who you want to be. Slowing down helps us determine our priorities, whether in the moment or more broadly.

Finally, remember that you will die. Morbid, I know. Sorry! But absolutely, 100 percent true. Nothing shifts your perspective faster than contemplating the mortality of you and everyone you care about. We can traffic in what Roman emperor-slash-Stoic philosopher Marcus Aurelius referred to as "everlasting grumbles." Or we can choose another attitude, such as one of gratitude. We can go slow and adore the boring (see axiom 28 on page 95). We can act deliberately and react appropriately. We can choose to change. We can choose joy.

BE MORE AXOLOTL

CULTURE

Simply by reading *The Little Book of Axolotl Wisdom*, you've taken an important first step in becoming more axolotl. But you can go even further by checking out these literary works, movies, and television shows.

An American Sunrise by Joy Harjo (2019)

In this book of poetry, former US poet laureate Joy Harjo describes the experiences of her family and the Mvskoke people, touching on tribal history as well as her involvement with the native rights movement.

The Big Lebowski (1998)

Is there any movie character more axolotl-like than "The Dude" (played by Jeff Bridges)? Maybe David Wooderson (played by Matthew McConaughey) in *Dazed and Confused* (1993). Watch both, and let me know.

Bird by Bird by Anne Lamott (1995)

Ostensibly a book about the craft of writing, this classic is beloved by writers and nonwriters alike for its practical wisdom, folksy positivity, and spirituality.

Hilda (2018–present)
Based on the graphic novels of the same name, the Netflix series *Hilda* follows an inquisitive, imaginative young girl and her pet deer-fox as they uncover secrets of the magical world around them. Like most kids, Hilda is never without a hefty dose of awe.

"Joy" by Zadie Smith (2013)
In this 2013 essay, originally published in *The New York Review of Books*, Zadie Smith draws a meaningful distinction between joy and pleasure. Life, luckily, offers plenty of opportunities for both.

Meditations by Marcus Aurelius (171–175 CE)
Written in the second century as a series of Stoic self-reminders, *Meditations* has endless, ageless applications to contemporary life, among them "be yourself" and "don't complain."

My Octopus Teacher (2020)
If you're at all skeptical about how we can learn resilience from animals, see axiom 12 on page 47). Then watch this documentary about the relationship that develops between a diver and a cephalopod.

Roma (2018)
Roma is writer-director Alfonso Cuarón's semiautobiographical, cinematic paean to his childhood, especially his mother and nanny. The movie simultaneously offers a view into 1970s-era Mexico City and taps into universal themes about love and family.

FAMOUS AXOLOTLS

Long a symbol in Mexican art and culture, axolotls continue to pop up in a variety of places, including Minecraft, the back of the 50-peso bill, and TikTok, where #axolotl has more than 2 billion views. Here are five of the most famous axolotls and axolotl-like characters around today.

Axolil, Pokémon

Given that the actual axolotl looks like a Pokémon, it shouldn't come as a surprise that there is, in fact, an axolotl Pokémon. Named Axolil, this tiny creature has psychic abilities and likes to hang out in its cave habitat.

Gary the Axolotl, YouTube

Giving Chonk (see axiom 4 on page 23) a run for the money, Gary the Axolotl is among the most well-known real-life axolotls. You can watch a livestream of Gary, along with his tankmate, Migi, 24 hours a day, seven days a week on YouTube. Check it out for a dose of Zen, or join Gary's Kingdom on Discord to connect with like-minded fans.

Toothless, *How to Train Your Dragon* (2010–present)

One of the stars of the *How to Train Your Dragon* series, Toothless is curious, spirited, and smart. While technically a "Night Fury" dragon, Toothless's adorable mien was based, in part, on that of an axolotl.

Unnamed Protagonist, "Axolotl" (1956)

In this surrealist short story by Julio Cortázar, the narrator goes from admiring axolotls as they swim around to transforming into one. Some critics see the work as representing Cortázar's struggles with his bicultural identity; others argue that it depicts the creative process.

Yolanda Buenaventura, *BoJack Horseman* (2014–2020)
An asexual axolotl, Yolanda Buenaventura begins dating Todd Chavez in season 4 of this cartoon dramedy. Other noteworthy characteristics include her professional attitude toward her job at the Better Business Bureau and utter immunity to Paul Rudd's charms.

ACTIVITIES

In addition to following our axolotl axioms, we can be more axolotl by trying different axolotl-like activities. Read on for details.

☐ **Dance:** In 2003, scientists discovered that dancing helps stave off dementia, on par with mental activities like reading and playing board games. Ergo, dancing is good for you. Axolotls dance before they mate (see axiom 21 on page 74).

☐ **Eat Some Gummy Worms:** Axolotls go in for all kinds of worms, especially earthworms and blackworms (see axiom 15 on page 56). In labs, they also eat brine shrimp, beef liver, and salmon pellets, in case any of those appeal to you.

☐ **Go Swimming:** Axolotls love the water. If you want to be more axolotl, you should, too. Axolotls prefer freshwater, but you can feel free to swim in the sea or a pool.

☐ **Learn about Land Acknowledgments:** Educate yourself about the Indigenous Peoples or Nations who lived in your hometown before colonization, genocide, or removal. Axolotls, for example, were important to the Aztec (Mexica).

- [ ] **Say "Derp":** If axolotls could speak, no doubt they'd pepper their speech with lingo like "chillaxification," "calm your farm," and "chilajate." Bonus if you follow your "derp" with "duuuuuuude."

- [ ] **Smile:** When you smile, your body releases "feel good" hormones like serotonin and dopamine (as we discuss in axiom 16 on page 59). An axolotl's near-constant smile makes it look goofy and blissed out.

- [ ] **Take Baths:** See "Go Swimming" above. Mimic the protective coat of mucus that covers an axolotl's skin using essential oils.

- [ ] **Zone Out:** Axolotls aren't into productivity or optimization via life hacks. To mimic their unblinking, zoned-out stare, try watching Gary the Axolotl's livestream on YouTube (see Famous Axolotls on page 109).

BE AN AXOLOTL (PET) PARENT

Axolotls make popular pets. Unlike dogs, they won't pee on the floor or hump your friend's leg. Unlike cats, they are not interested in dominating their human servants. Instead, they swim or walk around their tank, spreading good vibes and cuteness.

BASIC DOS & DON'TS FOR AXOLOTL PET PARENTS

DOS	DON'TS
☐ Use the right size tank (15–20 gallons)	☐ Put your axolotl in a tiny tank or goldfish bowl
☐ Keep your axolotl's tank clean	☐ Touch your axolotl with your bare hands
☐ Aim for one axolotl per tank	☐ Place multiple axolotls in the same tank
☐ Feed your axolotl appropriate food, such as earthworms and brine shrimp	☐ Feed your axolotl Cheetos, Skittles, or other junk food; skip other pet food, too
☐ Use filtered water	☐ Fill your tank with regular tap water
☐ Watch for danger signs like sluggishness, loss of appetite, or dry, flaky skin	☐ Ignore health problems
☐ Dedicate an Instagram account to your axolotl	☐ Put your phone into your axolotl's tank
☐ Photoshop photos of you and your axolotl cuddling, playing basketball, walking around Paris, etc.	☐ Take your axolotl out of its tank
☐ Enjoy your axolotl for years to come	☐ Release your axolotl into the wild

YOUR STATE'S LAWS

Some US states, including California and Virginia, ban axolotls as pets. Others require a permit, available through your city or state's health department or wildlife division. For the record, jaguars and chimpanzees are also banned, as are certain turtles, snakes, and birds.

In the case of axolotls, though, it's less about the danger of losing your face to a creature that is only partly domesticated and more about possible eco-destruction if your axolotl gets out and starts getting frisky with the locals. Pet axolotls are genetically different from wild axolotls, and both are different from other types of salamanders. While it's hard to imagine an adorable axolotl wreaking environmental havoc—how could something so charming be destructive?—the fact is that an escaped pet axolotl could potentially overwhelm a native species of amphibian. So do some research, including Googling "[your location] axolotl pet license," before purchasing a pet axolotl.

QUOTES

Reading these quotes will make you 1,000 times more axolotl.

♡ ♡ ♡

My father used to say, "Don't raise your voice; improve your argument."
—Archbishop Desmond Tutu

Tell me, what is it you plan to do / with your one wild and precious life?
—Mary Oliver

The way I see it, if you want the rainbow, you gotta put up with the rain.
—Dolly Parton

Gender and sexuality are so fluid—it's okay to change your mind a million times and figure out what works for you. It's okay to take your time.
—Amandla Stenberg

When you know better, you do better.
—Oprah Winfrey

Bad days happen to everyone, but when one happens to you, just keep doing your best and never let a bad day make you feel bad about yourself.
—Big Bird

You're a human being, you live once and life is wonderful, so eat the damn red velvet cupcake.
—Emma Stone

I took a deep breath and listened to the old brag of my heart. I am, I am, I am.

—Sylvia Plath

Do not be too timid and squeamish about your actions. All life is an experiment. The more experiments you make the better.

—Ralph Waldo Emerson

I don't want to be at the mercy of my emotions. I want to use them, to enjoy them, and to dominate them.

—Oscar Wilde

How we spend our days is, of course, how we spend our lives. What we do with this hour, and that one, is what we are doing.

—Annie Dillard

FINAL THOUGHTS

Unlike the axolotl, we can't regrow our brains. However, after 31 axolotl axioms, you've learned how to retrain your brain, trick your brain, and benefit your brain. You've heard from Marcus Aurelius, Joan Didion, and Amandla Stenberg, among others, and read summaries of some of the most influential scientific studies to date. You've learned how to be a better conversationalist, own your hard, know your needs, and harness your growth factor.

Growing is great. Definitely don't stop growing. You are a unique individual who has so much to offer and so much to contribute. But, even as you strive for self-improvement and cultivate a growth mindset, take time to focus on what's working. Try it! Close your eyes and picture your life. There's got to be at least one thing, maybe a thousand things, in your life that bring you joy, peace, and pride right now. Whoever you are, whatever you're struggling or dealing with, there's something about your life that's working. Hold onto it. Do more of it.

Remember that axolotls are cute, yet complex. They have goofy grins and giant genomes. They look like overgrown tadpoles and can repeatedly regrow parts of their bodies. Consider Kim Kardashian—reality star, mother, socialite, billionaire businessperson, model, *and* aspiring lawyer. She's not just one of those things;

THE LITTLE BOOK OF AXOLOTL WISDOM

she's all of them. Embrace the "and," and be more than the sum of your parts. Experiment. Try new things. Cultivate curiosity.

Be a good advocate for yourself. Be kind to yourself and to others. Especially to yourself. Make good choices. Avoid situations where you might be compelled to make bad choices. Take care of yourself. Accept yourself. Embrace your weird. Don't be afraid to ask for what you want—from a partner, from a family member, from an employer. Set goals. Volunteer. Reduce your impact on the planet. Underreact. Be generous. Be grateful. Stay hydrated. Be awed. Flip back to axolotl axiom 1: you are, after all, an effing miracle. Don't ever forget that.

I love you. Keep swimming.

WORKS CITED

Aurelius, Marcus. *Meditations*. Translated by Maxwell Staniforth. New York: Penguin Group, 2005.

Bryant, Erin. "Lack of Sleep in Middle Age May Increase Dementia Risk." National Institutes of Health, US Department of Health and Human Services, April 27, 2021. https://www.nih.gov/news -events/nih-research-matters/lack-sleep-middle-age-may -increase-dementia-risk.

Collins, Lauren. "Real Romance." *The New Yorker*, June 15, 2009. https://www.newyorker.com/magazine/2009/06/22/real- romance-2.

Cortázar, Julio. *End of the Game and Other Stories*. Translated by Paul Blackburn. New York: Harper & Row, 1978.

Craig, Anne. "Discovery of 'Thought Worms' Opens Window to the Mind." *Queen's Gazette*, July 13, 2020. https://www.queensu.ca /gazette/stories/discovery-thought-worms-opens-window-mind.

Curtin, Melanie. "Neuroscience Says Doing This 1 Thing Makes You Just as Happy as Eating 2,000 Chocolate Bars." *Inc.*, August 29, 2017. https://www.inc.com/melanie-curtin/science-says-doing -this-makes-you-just-as-happy-as.html.

de Both, N. J. "Transplantation of Axolotl Heads." *Science* 162, no. 3852 (October 25, 1968): 460–461. https://www.science.org/doi /epdf/10.1126/science.162.3852.460.

Deines, Tina. "Mexico City's Endangered Axolotl Has Found Fame— Is That Enough to Save It?" *National Geographic*, January 14,

THE LITTLE BOOK OF AXOLOTL WISDOM

2022. https://www.nationalgeographic.com/animals/article
/mexico-is-finally-embracing-its-quirky-salamander-the-axolotl.

Didion, Joan. *The White Album*. New York: Simon & Schuster, 1979.

Dillard, Annie. *The Writing Life*. New York: Harper & Row, 1989.

Eliot, T. S. "The Love Song of J. Alfred Prufrock." Poetry Foundation. Accessed March 20, 2022. https://www.poetryfoundation.org /poetrymagazine/poems/44212/the-love-song-of-j-alfred -prufrock.

Emerson, Ralph Waldo. *Journals and Miscellaneous Notebooks of Ralph Waldo Emerson*, vol. VII, 1838–1842. Quoted in *Great Occasions: Readings for the Celebration of Birth, Coming-of-Age, Marriage, and Death*, edited by C. Seaburg, 84. Boston: Skinner House Books, 1998.

Ericsson, K. A., R. T. Krampe, and C. Tesch-Römer. "The Role of Deliberate Practice in the Acquisition of Expert Performance." *Psychological Review* 100, no. 3 (1993): 363–406. https://doi.org /10.1037/0033-295X.100.3.363.

Fessl, Sophie. "The Race to Save the Axolotl." *JSTOR Daily*, April 25, 2018. https://daily.jstor.org/the-race-to-save-the-axolotl.

Fitzgerald, F. Scott. "The Crack-Up," *Esquire*, 1936. Excerpted in "S16 Ep2: F. Scott Fitzgerald: Winter Dreams," *American Masters*, PBS, August 31, 2005. https://www.pbs.org/wnet/americanmasters/f -scott-fitzgerald-essay-the-crack-up/1028/.

Granovetter, Mark S. "The Strength of Weak Ties." *American Journal of Sociology* 78, no. 6 (May 1973): 1360–1380. https://www.cse .wustl.edu/~m.neumann/fl2017/cse316/materials/strength_of _weak_ties.pdf.

Gray, James P. "It's a Gray Area: Einstein's Brilliant Thoughts Pertinent to Today's Woes." *Los Angeles Times*, May 31, 2013. https://www.latimes.com/socal/daily-pilot/opinion/tn-dpt-me -0602-gray-20130531-story.html.

Gutman, Ron. "The Hidden Power of Smiling." Filmed March 2011 at TED2011, Long Beach, California. Video, 7:10. https://www.ted .com/talks/ron_gutman_the_hidden_power_of_smiling.

Henderson, Caspar. *The Book of Barely Imagined Beings: A 21st Century Bestiary*. Chicago: University of Chicago Press, 2013.

Herhold, Leslie Theriot. *Self-Confidence Strategies for Women: Essential Tools to Increase Self-Esteem and Achieve Your True Potential*. Emeryville, CA: Rockridge Press, 2020.

Holt-Lunstad, Julianne, Timothy B. Smith, and J. Bradley Layton. "Social Relationships and Mortality Risk: A Meta-analytic Review." *PLOS* Medicine (July 27, 2010). https://doi.org/10.1371/journal .pmed.1000316.

Hugo, Kristin. "Extraordinary Salamander Can Grow New Limbs and Has Longest Genome Ever Sequenced." *Newsweek*, January 25, 2018. https://www.newsweek.com/axolotls-masters -regeneration-have-insanely-long-genomes-791052.

King, Stephen. *On Writing: A Memoir of the Craft*. New York: Scribner, 2000.

Learn, Joshua Rapp. "Complete Axolotl Genome Could Reveal the Secret of Regenerating Tissues." *Smithsonian*, January 24, 2019. https://www.smithsonianmag.com/science-nature/complete -axolotl-genome-could-reveal-secret-regenerating-tissues -180971335/.

Lee, Lewina O., Peter James, Emily S. Zevon, Eric S. Kim, Claudia Trudel-Fitzgerald, Avron Spiro III, Francine Grodstein, and Laura D. Kubzansky. "Optimism Is Associated with Exceptional Longevity in 2 Epidemiologic Cohorts of Men and Women." *PNAS* 116, no. 37 (August 26, 2019): 18357–18362. https://doi.org/10.1073 /pnas.1900712116.

McNiece, Mia. "Samuel L. Jackson on His Addiction Battle and How His Family's Love Changed His Life." *People*, March 16, 2022.

https://people.com/movies/samuel-l-jackson-on-his-addiction
-battle-and-how-his-familys-love-changed-his-life.

"Mexico's 'Water Monster' the Axolotl May Have Vanished from
Natural Habitat." *The Guardian*, January 29, 2014. https://www
.theguardian.com/environment/2014/jan/29/mexico-water
-monster-axolotl-vanished.

Mosely, Rachel. "Amandla Stenberg on Being Proud of Her Sexuality."
Seventeen, September 19, 2018. https://www.seventeen.com
/celebrity/a23287170/amandla-stenberg-on-being-proud-of-her
-sexuality.

Nestor, James. *Breath: The New Science of a Lost Art*. New York:
Riverhead Books, 2020.

Obama, Michelle. *Becoming*. New York: Crown Publishing Group,
2018.

O'Connell, Caitlin. *Wild Rituals: 10 Lessons Animals Can Teach Us
about Connection, Community, and Ourselves*. San Francisco:
Chronicle Books, 2021.

O'Connell, Rebecca. "11 Awesome Axolotl Facts." *Mental Floss*, April
16, 2015. https://www.mentalfloss.com/article/63130/11-awesome
-axolotl-facts.

Oliver, Mary. "Poem 133: The Summer Day." *Poetry 180*, Library of
Congress. Accessed March 5, 2022. https://www.loc.gov
/programs/poetry-and-literature/poet-laureate/poet-laureate
-projects/poetry-180/all-poems/item/poetry-180-133/the-
summer-day.

Parton, Dolly (@DollyParton). "The way I see it, if you want the
rainbow, you gotta put up with the rain." Twitter, March 24, 2020.
https://twitter.com/dollyparton/status/1242587160525647872.

Plath, Sylvia. *The Bell Jar*. New York: Harper & Row, 1971.

Preston, Elizabeth. "Salamander's Genome Guards Secrets of Limb
Regrowth." *Quanta Magazine*, July 7, 2018. Republished in

Scientific American. Accessed April 9, 2022. https://www
.scientificamerican.com/article/salamander-rsquo-s-genome
-guards-secrets-of-limb-regrowth.

Proyer, René. "A New Structural Model for the Study of Adult
Playfulness: Assessment and Exploration of an Understudied
Individual Differences Variable." *Personality and Individual
Differences* 108 (April 2017):113–122. https://doi.org/10.1016/j.paid
.2016.12.011.

Rosen, Michael J. *Outrageous Animal Adaptations: From Big-Eared
Bats to Frill-Necked Lizards*. Minneapolis, MN: Twenty-First
Century Books, 2018.

Rudd, Melanie, Kathleen D. Vohs, and Jennifer Aaker. "Awe Expands
People's Perception of Time, Alters Decision Making, and
Enhances Well-Being." *Psychological Science* 23, no. 10 (2012):
1130–1136. https://www.bauer.uh.edu/mrrudd/download
/AweExpandsTimeAvailability.pdf.

Sarner, Lauren. "'Sesame Street' 50th Anniversary: The Best
Character Quotes Ever." *New York Post*, November 6, 2019.
https://nypost.com/2019/11/06/sesame-street-50th-anniversary
-the-best-character-quotes-ever.

Schipani, Sam. "How to Save the Paradoxical Axolotl." *Smithsonian*,
January 8, 2018. https://www.smithsonianmag.com/science
-nature/saving-paradoxical-axolotl-180967734.

Schoch, Rainer R., Ralf Werneburg, and Sebastian Voigt. "A
Triassic Stem-Salamander from Kyrgyzstan and the Origin of
Salamanders." *PNAS* 117, no. 21 (May 11, 2020): 11584–11588.
https://doi.org/10.1073/pnas.2001424117.

Sel, Alejandra, Beatriz Calvo-Merino, Simone Tuettenberg, and
Bettina Forster. "When You Smile, The World Smiles at You: ERP
Evidence for Self-Expression Effects on Face Processing." *Social
Cognitive and Affective Neuroscience* 10, no. 10 (October 2015):
1316–1322. https://doi.org/10.1093/scan/nsv009.

Selig, Mark. "Michael Jordan's Top 23 Commercials, Remembered and Ranked." *The Washington Post,* April 27, 2020. https://www.washingtonpost.com/sports/2020/04/27/michael-jordan-commercials/.

Shire, Warsan. "Difficult Names." Quoted in Amanda Hess, "Warsan Shire, the Woman Who Gave Poetry to Beyoncé's 'Lemonade,'" *The New York Times*, April 27, 2016. https://www.nytimes.com/2016/04/28/arts/music/warsan-shire-who-gave-poetry-to-beyonces-lemonade.html.

Simon, Matt. *The Wasp That Brainwashed the Caterpillar: Evolution's Most Unbelievable Solutions to Life's Biggest Problems.* New York: Penguin Books, 2016.

Spencer, Amy. "Emma Stone: The Cool Girl." *Glamour*, March 28, 2011. https://www.glamour.com/story/emma-stone-the-cool-girl.

Stellar, J. E., N. John-Henderson, C. L. Anderson, A. M. Gordon, G. D. McNeil, and D. Keltner. "Positive Affect and Markers of Inflammation: Discrete Positive Emotions Predict Lower Levels of Inflammatory Cytokines." *Emotion* 15, no. 2 (2015): 129–133. https://doi.org/10.1037/emo0000033.

Stoffel, Jaclyn M., and Jeff Cain. "Review of Grit and Resilience Literature Within Health Professions Education." *American Journal of Pharmaceutical Education* 82, no. 2 (March 2018): 6150. https://www.ncbi.nlm.nih.gov/pmc/articles/PMC5869747/.

Syme, Rachel. "In 'Russian Doll,' Natasha Lyonne Barrels into the Past." *The New Yorker*, April 11, 2022.

Tutu, Archbishop Desmond. "The Second Nelson Mandela Annual Lecture Address," November 23, 2004, Nelson Mandela Foundation. https://www.nelsonmandela.org/news/entry/the-second-nelson-mandela-annual-lecture-address.

Vance, Erik. "Biology's Beloved Amphibian—the Axolotl—Is Racing Towards Extinction." *Nature*, November 15, 2017. https://www.nature.com/articles/d41586-017-05921-w.

Voss, S. Randal, M. Ryan Woodcock, and Luis Zambrano. "A Tale of Two Axolotls." *BioScience* 65, no. 12 (December 1, 2015): 1134–1140. https://doi.org/10.1093/biosci/biv153.

Water Science School. "The Water in You: Water and the Human Body." US Geological Survey. May 22, 2019. https://www.usgs.gov/special-topics/water-science-school/science/water-you-water-and-human-body.

Wilde, Oscar. *The Picture of Dorian Gray*. Project Gutenberg. Accessed April 21, 2022. https://www.gutenberg.org/files/174/174-h/174-h.htm.

Wilmot, Michael P. and Deniz S. Ones. "A Century of Research on Conscientiousness at Work." *PNAS* 116, no. 46 (October 30, 2019): 23004–23010. https://doi.org/10.1073/pnas.1908430116.

Winfrey, Oprah. "The Powerful Lesson Maya Angelou Taught Oprah." *The Oprah Winfrey Show*. Aired on October 19, 2011. Video, 4:16. https://www.oprah.com/oprahs-lifeclass/the-powerful-lesson-maya-angelou-taught-oprah-video.

Wu, Tim. "In Praise of Mediocrity." *The New York Times*, September 29, 2018. https://www.nytimes.com/2018/09/29/opinion/sunday/in-praise-of-mediocrity.html.

Yin, Steph (Feini). "Seeking Superpowers in the Axolotl Genome." *The New York Times*, January 29, 2019. https://www.nytimes.com/2019/01/29/science/axolotl-dna-genome-sequence.html.

Zambrano, Luis. "A Lotl Love for the Axolotl." Interview by Maddie Sofia, Berly Mccoy, and Emily Kwong. *Short Wave*. NPR, September 16, 2021. Podcast audio, 12:00. https://www.npr.org/transcripts/1036590555.

MORE RESOURCES

Axolotl.org
A good first port of call, this site got its start in 1998. It's filled with details about keeping axolotls at home, information about basic biology and genetics, and links to other sites and discussion groups for hobbyists and enthusiasts, including an active board devoted to axolotls.

Herpetology Hotline
ssarherps.org/all-about-herps/herpetology-hotline

Organized by the Society for the Study of Amphibians and Reptiles, and staffed by volunteers from museums, government wildlife agencies, and universities, this email helpline can help solve your hardest herpetology conundrums.

National Amphibian Conservation Center at the Detroit Zoo
detroitzoo.org/animal-habitat/national-amphibian-conservation
-center

On display at the National Amphibian Conservation Center, part of the Detroit Zoo, are more than 1,000 amphibians from around the globe, letting visitors experience these creatures in an array of diverse habitats, with a focus on caring, protecting, and promoting animals.

Planet Possible

natgeo.com/planetpossible

Launched to commemorate Earth Day 2021, this multiplatform initiative specializes in noteworthy news concerning our very own Blue Marble, from amazing animals to incredible individuals to actionable conservation information.

Zoology: Inside the Secret World of Animals (2019)

amazon.com/Zoology-Inside-Secret-World-Animals/dp /1465482512

All kinds of amazing animals live on earth. Page through this lavishly photographed book, coproduced between the publisher DK and the Smithsonian Institution, to learn about the anatomy, behavior, defense mechanisms, mating rituals, and environment of myriad magnificent creatures.

ACKNOWLEDGMENTS

Thank you to the scientists, environmentalists, conservationists, researchers, and all the other folks on the front lines of learning more about, and caring for, our planet in an effort to make sure it's habitable for axolotl (and human) generations to come. A million thanks, too, to everyone at Ulysses Press, especially Claire Sielaff and Cathy Cambron. Kristine Byun and Winnie Liu, your illustrations are wonderful. Hat tip to New York City, my beloved adopted hometown, which never ceases to nurture my awe. And extra special thanks—as well as endless gratitude and boundless love—go to my husband and our precious offspring. You two are my life. Let's go have an adventure!

ABOUT THE AUTHOR

Jessica Allen has written for *The Boston Globe*, CNN, *The Independent*, McSweeney's, Mental Floss, *The Washington Post*, *Writer's Digest*, and many other publications. Based in New York City, she's swum with humpback whales in the South Pacific and chased after chimpanzees in Uganda, fed elephants in Laos and sung along with howler monkeys in Nicaragua. But her favorite animal encounter, by far, is hanging out with her husband and son.